The Entrepreneur Roadmap

The Entrepreneur Roadmap

Published by THNQ Global Corp, June, 2021
ISBN: 9781777748401

Typeset: Greg Salisbury & Colin Christensen
Book Cover Design: Colin Christensen
Portrait Photographer: MapleBee Photos

DISCLAIMER: This is a work of non-fiction. The information is of a general nature to help you on the subject of business. Readers of this publication agree that neither Colin Christensen, nor his publisher will be held responsible or liable for damages that may be alleged or resulting directly or indirectly from their use of this publication. All external links are provided as a resource only and are not guaranteed to remain active for any length of time. Neither the publisher nor the author can be held accountable for the information provided by, or actions resulting from accessing these resources.

Praise for The Entrepreneur Roadmap and the author

The Entrepreneur Roadmap is a fantastic training system with valuable tools for developing a company, whether a startup in the earliest stages, or a mature company trying to figure out where to grow next. This system is steadily becoming a global standard.
-- Travis – seasoned entrepreneur

All of this made a tremendous difference. I'm grateful I got to meet and have input, because of how much it has benefited me. I look at the notes from our meeting on a regular basis. I've shown my team members too! Because of this, I could go into the process willing to work hard, make mistakes, pick myself up and start the process all over again. It became an exciting experience for me.
-- Manny – new entrepreneur

Colin is a born entrepreneur, personable, funny, driven, and a voracious learner. He strives to be better for himself, his clients and his family, on so many levels. Colin dreams without fear and tackles challenges with confidence. He understands business and loves to share his knowledge and mentor others. I respect Colin not only for his business savvy but for his core values and the intense loyalty he shows those in his inner circle
-- Bridget – colleague

Colin helped us think critically about the future of our business. It was the best strategic planning session we've had.
-- Lorne – seasoned entrepreneur

I don't think my brain has ever had this much of a workout and it was one of the greatest experiences of my life. Colin took someone with no business experience, just an idea and determination and gave me the tools I needed to turn it into a successful business.
-- Mitch – emerging entrepreneur

Colin did an amazing job coaching me to organize my thoughts for a pitching competition, he helped me to make our story flowing well for everyone to understand the journey our company has gone through.
-- Mina – Winner of a provincial pitch competition

I attended Colin's 4 classes for creating a business, and with his help, we were able to point out some "blind spots" that I overlooked and helped me work through the hurdles. Without Colin's guidance, I would have made some very costly errors that were very easily diverted by having another set of eyes, and years of knowledge to guide me.
-- Jeremy – emerging entrepreneur

I have known Colin for more than 10 years and have always found that he has added value to me in my endeavors. The Entrepreneur Roadmap has taken it to the next level. It is a great resource for anyone who is looking to become more successful. Great work, Colin!
-- Steve – seasoned entrepreneur

I benefited 10x more from this one meeting with you compared to my whole last year with another mentor
-- Nick – established entrepreneur

Colin facilitated a weekend entrepreneur bootcamp. I gained a magnitude of knowledge from him and the materials that he shared with us during the short conference (dare I say, even more than in the business classes I have taken at the university), in regard to not only startups and how to help your business succeed, but how to read people and communicate with them effectively. Colin walked with us through the creation of our entire business plan model and provided fantastic feedback and suggestions along the way in a professional and constructive manner. I would highly recommend Entrepreneur Roadmap to anyone with any concerns regarding the direction of their business.
-- Kimberly – student entrepreneur

Like any master of their craft, Colin was able to quickly distill a complex narrative into its core values and message. His insights were on the mark and his support was invaluable. I highly recommend him for any marketing, branding, or strategy. Thanks again!
-- Matt – seasoned entrepreneur

I think going through this process has made me a better planner and I know what I need to do to get my business off the ground.
-- Sarah – student entrepreneur

My mentor has become like a sister to me. I wanted to quit multiple times but she wanted this for me as well. I see myself differently now and she never sugar coated anything which is what I needed and helped make the entrepreneurial lifestyle very realistic. Overall a wonderful person and my experience wouldn't have been the same without her.
-- Cathy – student entrepreneur

Loved the tools, they were a great way to evaluate and progress through my idea, putting into words important steps, and asking key questions to see the validation in progressing an idea.
-- Brent – seasoned entrepreneur

I had fun and I was pushed to break out of my shell. I would have never done something like this and I'm glad more people can participate in this program in the future.
-- Anyieth – student entrepreneur

---- INDUSTRY

Colin did an amazing speaking engagement job facilitating our Entrepreneur Guest Speaking & Networking event. He was very professional and engaging. Our start-ups indicated "they valued the opportunity to learn from Colin." Many thanks and keep your great job, Colin!
-- Abdoulaye - Local organization helping immigrant Entrepreneurs (Colin ended up facilitating a full 14 week program for them)

Most entrepreneurs that do not succeed on their first effort do not make the attempt to try again. They may later learn that the first "failure" was only part of their early education. The Entrepreneur Roadmap is providing valuable education for these first-time entrepreneurs. It is our expectation that this education will not only cause a higher rate of first-time success but more importantly a higher rate of entrepreneurs willing to return to their startup ambitions for a second try. It is our experience that a tested entrepreneur in a second pursuit can be of tremendous value.

-- Warren Bergen, President, AVAC (VC)

I was able to sit in on Colin's Entrepreneur Roadmap session this last weekend and was really impressed and got a ton of value going through his framework. He was able to simplify the process into bite sized pieces that were engaging and interesting. Colin is a great facilitator that truly loves what he does, and loves helping others... That was very obvious. I look forward to crossing paths with Colin again!

-- Tim – seasoned entrepreneur

We recently had a workshop that was catered towards new graduates and young professionals and had the pleasure of having Colin run the workshop for us. He presented the information in a way that was very approachable and relatable. His professionalism and motivating energy in his delivery also contributed to the great success of the event. He would make a great mentor to any professional or entrepreneur seeking his expertise.

-- Amie - Mentoring Organization

Colin did an amazing job facilitating our Entrepreneur Roadmap event. He was very professional and engaging. Participants said they appreciated the opportunity to learn from him. Thank you Colin!

-- Krystal – Organizer for a regionalized weekend bootcamp

Colin Christensen is an entrepreneur who gives back to the Edmonton innovation community. His generosity of time and insight is so well received by the entrepreneurs. For the whole 15-year program, he volunteered as a mentor, screener and judge for the annual TEC Venture Prize competition. He always shows up when called upon to help entrepreneurs. He provides our community with workshops and helps founders with honing their pitching skills. Colin is a valuable and impactful member in the Edmonton entrepreneurial community and always ready to share his knowledge.

-- Lan - TEC Edmonton

Introduction

This book is part manual, part inspiration: inspirational as in, "Wow, I can do this" and "If he can do it, so can I." A practical manual as in, "This is simple enough that I can remember and implement it in my business (and life for that matter)." Still, it should be deep enough that it can be useful and powerful for the leader of the largest businesses.

I have been in and around business my whole life and have seen wild ups and downs. As I built my own businesses, I would reflect to learn lessons as things happened. As well, I would read. I've read a lot. I try to synthesize information and put pieces together in my mind. I try to value and curate them like a wine connoisseur who listens to someone looking for the right wine to pair with a certain meal. I've learned to suggest the right management tool at the right time for the right person, trying to get them unstuck and more successful.

One of my gifts is being able to see elements from multiple directions at one time. Maybe I can help you develop that skill.

Try this exercise: There is a 3D shape that fits through each of these spaces perfectly. What is it?

This exercise illustrates a skill you need: to be able to see things from different angles.

My high school drafting teacher posed this problem to the class. I instantly knew the solution. I took a small piece of chalk, filed down two sides, and to his surprise, I got it right.

This guides me as an entrepreneur. When "it" doesn't work, I don't give up. I just try to see "it" from a different perspective.

This manual helps the entrepreneur be prepared to answer the questions about themselves and their business that they really need to know. I aim to help entrepreneurs build the tools that seasoned entrepreneurs have learned so they can avoid failure. Seeing a problem from a new perspective means not repeating the same errors endlessly, or not just giving up.

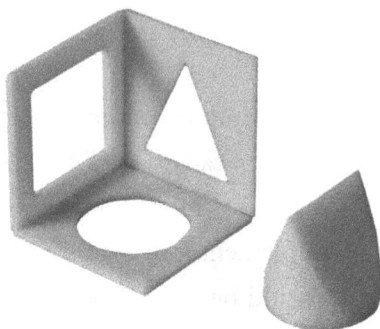

There are a few constructs I find important:

1. Avoiding needless failure. If I could wave a magic wand, I would want entrepreneurs to know when it's a good idea to quit. And balancing healthy quitting with tenacity.
2. Clarity over certainty. We can't be certain. We can grow clarity. The more we understand, the better decisions we make.

My audience is all entrepreneurs. You could be considering a business, maybe just starting out, or you could be someone seasoned and looking for an exit into retirement. We all need that little extra to solve the problem we're facing at the time.

Entrepreneurship can be lonely. One study showed that 2/3 of all entrepreneurs have some form of mental health issue. I have even read about entrepreneurs who take their own life. It's not just failure that leads to serious problems. It can be success with its attendant loneliness, the workload, or being the lightning rod for problems and blame. Later, I will share my own story with some epic failures and successes.

There is, of course, so much more to life than our business. Entrepreneurship is awesome. It can be fun, endlessly rewarding in success, but soul-crushing in its defeat. However, entrepreneurship is still just a single aspect of life. The purpose of our lives is much bigger than the business we start.

***

You will find references to many of my favourite writers throughout this book. Sometimes I refer to them directly; sometimes I can't remember where I got the idea. Everything I have developed is built on the shoulders of giants.

Here are a few of my giants: Warren Bergen, Henry Cloud, Jim Collins, Peter Drucker, Gordon Ferguson, Michael E Gerber, Malcolm Gladwell, Seth Godin, Daniel Harkavy, Verne Harnish, Michael Hyatt, Austin Kleon, Kouzes and Posner, Patrick Lencioni, John Maxwell, Geoff McKeown, Michael Michalowicz, Cal Newport, Daniel Pink, Dave Ramsay, Simon Sinek, Andy Stanley, Jeff Walker, Michael Walsh, Gino Wickman. From the Bible: David, Solomon, Paul, James, and others. I encourage you to read everything by these people. You will be happy you did.

Outline

The Foundation

A memory of the early appeal of entrepreneurship: I was at my grandparents' house in Ottawa, Ontario, about ten years old. There were not many kids my age in the neighbourhood so I was bored.

I drew to pass the time. I would draw almost anything I saw, and found joy in noticing how it took art to create everything, from my favourite cereal boxes to the Giles comic books my grandpa had lying everywhere. Not just the art fascinated me, but the design: the frames, the fonts, the layout, and the logos.

One day, that pivotal day, I announced: "I want to run my own graphic design company." Where did I hear the term "graphic design?" I don't even know where I got the idea of running a company; nonetheless, the goal was established.

After a period of troubled teens and a few extra-legal businesses, I realized that trying to get my dreamed-of Lamborghini through that type of business wasn't a clever idea. So, at twenty-three, I started my own graphic design company, working at it for about ten years. That has evolved over the last thirty years into my business today.

But first, I had some learning to do about the concept of "work." My mom lived with a man who owned a fishing lodge in Northern Ontario – and I got to observe their business. They would work eighteen plus hour days, seven days a week. from May until late September, then, apart from attending a few sports shows and cutting ice for the summer icehouse, they would take the winter off. I would join them after school ended in June and work those same hours with them until late

August when I returned to school.

I learned the value of ~~thankless labour~~ hard work as I served my time for those two months. The last year I was there I got paid $250. That works out to about 19¢/hour for that one year.

My jobs would range from digging outhouse holes to falling, splitting, and stacking trees to building log cabins to cleaning up after the twelve Huskies to cleaning and fileting the dozens of fish that customers brought in a couple times a day.

You can see why, in high school, I began questioning the idea of "working," of trading dollars for hours to help someone else get their business done.

My dad's experience was instructional, too. He worked for a few big food companies and finished his BSc in Chemistry while working full-time. Then, in the mid-eighties – along with countless others across the economy – he was fired. How did his hard work payoff for him?

Still, with my passion to work for myself, and the appeal of that dreamed-of Lamborghini pictured on my wall, I foolishly tried Amway. I am grateful for all the incredible lessons in business but I worked my butt off for a year or two and had nothing to show for it – aside from empty pockets and many friends who might have been avoiding me.

Then I became branch manager for a small business doing telemarketing to sell frozen meats and goods, dry foods, and a freezer if needed. The amazing thing: my branch grew, we duplicated the process four more times and the company went from three employees to forty in just two years. There were awards, galas, lollipops, and – for me – a lot of burnout. Shortly afterwards, I left the company.

Several years earlier, I had started that graphic design business of my dreams. Now, I gave it my full attention, designing logos and printing annual reports, even did contract production work for a kids' digital educational game. I worked through nights, slept under desks, and lived off some of the most memorable pizza ever. After turning out two award-winning kids' educational CD-ROM games, we were romanced then dropped by Microsoft. My last paycheque as we cleared out the office upon the collapse of the company: a TV and VCR.

My life wasn't all "work," though. I fell in love with and married my best friend. We've had challenges: four different jobs in one year, the stress of building a start-up, living through a market crash, then finding we were pregnant with a son who wouldn't live past birth. But the challenges have brought more love and more strength to our relationship over the twenty-four years.

One day, early in our marriage, a young man asked me to interview as a Recruiter. He said I had a great mix of entrepreneurship, sales, and technology.

"What's a Recruiter?" I asked.

For the next seven years, through Y2K, the dotcom era, 9/11, a huge boom in Alberta, I recruited, often with great success. I escaped just before The Great Recession.

In the meantime, my wife Melissa and I decided to move to Edmonton to help start a new church for the Christian group we were a part of. As we were settling in, we found out we were pregnant with another son.

The beck and call of entrepreneurship always wafted through the deeply enjoyable world I was working in. One night, after

I awoke refreshed with only a few hours' sleep, I did some research into sleep cycles and stumbled on a new invention called SleepTracker. It tracked sleep patterns and woke you up at the optimum time. I phoned the inventor and negotiated the Canadian Distribution Rights. Over the next few years, we saw SleepTracker on the list of Time Magazine's best inventions of 2005; Dr. Phil also did a show on it.

At the peak of it all, I was introduced to an opportunity for a golf franchise; I was fortunate enough to raise $100,000 in thirty days, using it to buy the rights across three provinces and start the plans for the first location.

Over the course of the next year, we raised over a million dollars. I quit my job because I could no longer manage both the golf franchise business and a full-time recruiting career. The best-timed exit I ever made was in the middle of 2007, out of recruiting. By late 2008, recruiting was never to be the same.

With the large sum of money we had raised, we started construction on the first location, even though we did not have all the money required. This was my biggest mistake.

For the next eighteen months, upon the promise of funds from our HQ, we went hard into raising more capital, growing pre-opening memberships, and continuing the build. And managing a growing list of debtors.

Our debts grew as we burned through investment dollars. Without a salary, my personal debt grew as well. Having to manage credit card collections, utility collections, landlords and mortgage lenders, as well as the rising expectations of the investors became a full-time job.

Through all of this, there were continued promises from our

HQ, from different types of investors, and from some promising speculative investors. The promises from our HQ fell through as they fell into dissolution which inevitably dragged us along. In the end, we had raised about $4,500,000 worth of investment and had nothing to show for it but a mostly-built location and no equipment.

Eventually, with spent hopes and no leads left, we packed it all in. My investors urged me to stop pushing a dead horse and go get a job to take care of my family. So, I did.

In the last days of dealing with this, on top of everything else, I somehow managed to contract Flesh Eating Disease. At first, it almost killed me. After three months of hospital stays, massive rounds of antibiotic cocktails, and several surgeries, however, I won.

Somehow, that last year, we were able to keep our family – now five of us - alive on under $20,000. We went from a new minivan and a BMW X5 to borrowing a friend's abandoned and barely running manual VW Golf with a two-foot hole in the passenger side floor.

In the end, I had no other choice but to declare bankruptcy. A year later, we lost the house through foreclosure.

The next four years were a blur: trying to build a side hustle, trying to earn enough to survive with my family of three growing kids, and working at anything I could. I searched on Fiverr and TaskRabbit. I tried Uber (my car was too old), and looked at hundreds of different roles that I was "overqualified" for. I tried roles with tire companies, oil change places, anything that might have a reasonable schedule. I even tried warehouse work at a temp agency but my bum ankle hurt so badly I couldn't walk after work.

Let's talk about something here for a minute: there is this stench that you feel you walk around with after a business disaster like that. You feel broken, or at least, incompetent. There is this battle that goes on in your head wondering if you're able to overcome it.

I also wrestled with destiny in the sense of wondering what I was going to do now, or what I was even good at. I thought I knew my talents, but without that "thing" to apply them to, I wasn't sure.

One more mind wrench: I'm a deeply Christian guy and it was clear to me God opened the doors when I started all this and then it seemed they were slammed shut once I was firmly inside. Many hours were spent in prayer and wrestling with God, trying to understand why this happened. It was a six-year wrestling match. I don't have all the answers, but I do have a few. Because hindsight is close to 20/20, I've written this Roadmap to help out entrepreneurs like you.

I finally got a break when an acquaintance who owned a trucking company was willing to let me work with a two-hour break in the middle of each day to meet with client prospects for my own business. There was another major benefit to the driving job: I was able to drive around and listen to podcasts and audiobooks all day. I consumed massive amounts of information, and it is a bit of an addiction to this day. This learning was a huge game changer in my mentality, my abilities, and my education.

After a year, I secured a client who paid me double the money compared to the driving job for one quarter of the time.

That client brought mixed emotions. The business owner

wanted help but wasn't willing to make the needed changes. For a year I worked with her to change all I could in her business. What I did not do, however, was work diligently to build other clients. When my one engagement ended, I was out of work again. Fortunately, I had almost three months of expenses saved up, and I worked hard getting new clients, at first one, then another, and more after that.

Today, things are cranking along. I often take on one or two excellent clients whom I love working with, and they keep telling me they love the impact I'm making in their lives and businesses. I also now run a business accelerator and incubator called Fuse42; we have launched a crowd-funding, micro-lending program and App partnering with HOPE Worldwide called LendHOPE that is expanding globally and looking to end poverty. We built a global team working on helping municipalities get off the grid through renewable energy solutions, and are inventing a new form of drywall to be naturally fire-resistant, mold-resistant, and lighter weight. I feel I have achieved that urge from my childhood to work for myself, enjoying all of my successes, and learning from each of my failures.

Now I couldn't care less if I have the Lamborghini. I continue to curate those experiences and lessons to give back to those entrepreneurs around me. What keeps me going is my passion to help entrepreneurs like you avoid needless failure. I hope these lessons help you become a difference maker in your own life, your family, and your community. This is the power of entrepreneurship.

The Entrepreneur Roadmap Tools

The Entrepreneur Roadmap, the ROOT App, and all the supporting tools can be found at http://EntrepreneurRoadmap. ca/.

Some of the tools merely need an explanation. Some require more coaching while you are using them. Each tool we talk about here will have a QR code to bring up a worksheet while you are reading about it. With the purchase of this book, you have one free year access to the tools. Use the code "TERMbook" for this access.

Being an entrepreneur is like walking down a street that has a big black pit in the middle. It is practically impossible not to fall in. Once in there, you have to grope around until you determine a way out, finding a foothold here, a jump to the left there, and a lot of good timing everywhere.

The holes are unavoidable. What is needed is a guide, someone who has seen the holes and been through enough of them to help you get out faster and safer. That's me - along with other experienced entrepreneurs in your circle.

I haven't been in every hole, nor do I want to, but from being around business my whole life, I have put together a pretty good map – if not to avoid the holes – at least not to fall too deeply and not to take too long to get out. We could call them hacks or shortcuts. The idea is, what are the 20% of activities that, if done right, will result in 80% of the successes?

Call the problems holes or unexpected bombs going off - it is what we don't know that kills us. This graphic is a reminder of the potential for surprise.

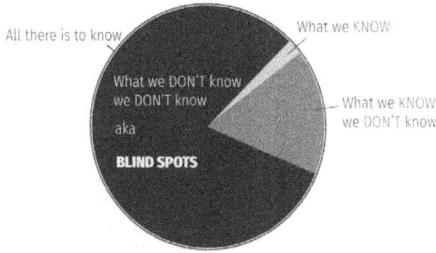

This roadmap is designed to ask questions that you never thought to ask, and frankly, should be able to answer. They should cause you to go, "Hmm, I don't know the answer to that," and then motivate you to research and think through an answer.

I often see my audience in three different groups. While there is much overlap, here are the basic groups: Early Entrepreneurs, Emerging Entrepreneurs, and Established Entrepreneurs.

Early Entrepreneurs: first-time entrepreneurs or those eager to get it right this time.

It's tough to get a business right the first time. Business failure happens, and it is important not to get discouraged by it. My advice: fail small and pivot – try again.

Emerging Entrepreneurs: those who have started a few businesses or have been in business for five plus years and have a revenue-generating business with several to dozens of employees.

Established Entrepreneurs: those who have run a mature business for more than a decade, and now are looking for an exit. Or, they might have several businesses with hundreds of employees and just love to build and flip businesses.

If you are in either of the last two categories, you could start with a review of the Q20 health checkup found through this

QR code. It will give you a good overview of elements in this book that will be most important.

This model, The Entrepreneur Roadmap, works for people at all three levels, although the execution of the plan may be a little different for each.

It is divided into two parts - Create and Improve - and is also a lemniscate, an infinity loop. Once you go through it all, go back to the beginning and continue to tighten it up over time in your business.

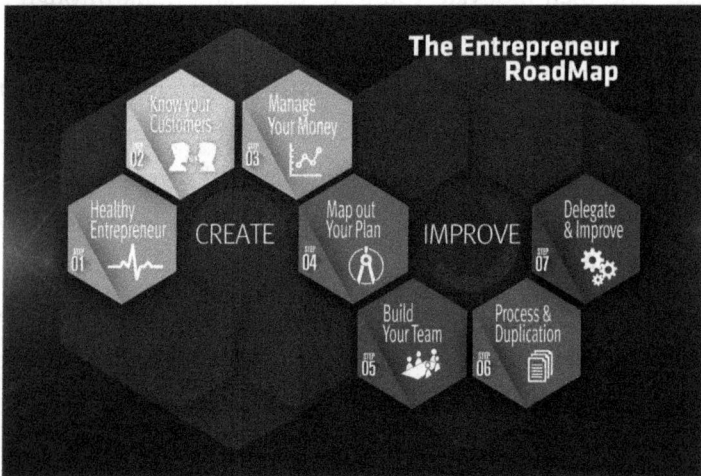

Entrepreneurs going through the Entrepreneur Roadmap will have answered many important questions and be better prepared for the help of investors, a marketing company, or any service provider.

Part I – Create

This is where any business can start. Even established businesses will benefit from starting right in the beginning.

When Part I is done well, you will have clear statements around Vision, Mission, Values and Goals. I call these the CORE of the business. Like a healthy body, your core is important. It stabilizes and helps all the rest of the parts work better and more efficiently. A healthy body is attractive, lives longer, it has more agility and flexibility, it recovers faster, is more resilient, and is easier to maintain. It is also more fun for the owner.

Vision: what you want to be when you grow up. A defined goal that tells the world you won. Imagine it as the Superbowl. It takes time to get there, maybe five or ten or even fifty years for some.

Mission: who you serve and how you serve them. The Mission is the group of people you are trying to please – your audience. It will include what you do to please or serve that audience.

Values: what you are willing to stand for and what you are not willing to stand for. A long-time client of Southwest Airlines, a business with a core value of "Fun," complained about the lack of seriousness around the safety demonstration exercise. The complaint made it all the way to CEO Herb Kelleher's desk. Kelleher wrote back four words: "We will miss you." He understood that a core value is not to be compromised.

Goals: the "plays" that move you toward your Vision. Keep achieving goals in a strategic fashion and you will succeed. Goals are your 90-day projects.

Part II – Improve

Many people will get a business going but then not mature it. The Improve part is about following your roadmap, heading in the direction you need to go. And then improving it. Improving your team, building processes, learning to delegate and constantly refining.

Let's begin by Creating.

PART I – CREATE

STEP 01 - Healthy Entrepreneur

This section deals with what it takes mentally to be an entrepreneur.

Being an entrepreneur is deeply satisfying and, at times, deeply soul-crushing. Yet, we always seem to answer the question "How's it going?" with "Awesome!" whether it is or isn't.

The problem is that if the business isn't doing awesome, we don't always feel awesome and, therefore, may be lying.

At a deeper level, this lying can lead to depression and, in extreme cases, entrepreneur suicide. The only way to get around this is by understanding that your business – any business – is just part of your big picture. Your business does not define who you are. It is separate.

I like to look at the entrepreneur as the driver and the business as the vehicle. A vehicle may fail, but the driver can get a better vehicle. Both can improve. You are more permanent and important than your vehicle in the big picture.

I am not advocating a flippant attitude towards business. In fact, without focus, determination, hard work, creativity and some luck, you will not succeed. However, when business has the right focus in your life, it becomes more of a joy and allows for the proper balance in all areas of your life.

To complete this section, I suggest you book some "me-time" in your schedule to get away from it all and shut off your connections to the outside world. Expect to spend about half a day or more working through this step.

Entrepreneur Assessment

One of my roles has me running a Business Accelerator. Entrepreneurs from around the world come looking for help and support financially through investment and help for their team and business to scale rapidly. We have a number of tools to ascertain where they are starting. One of them is a tool called the Entrepreneur Assessment. You might like it too.

It will give you hints on who you are as well as a document to share with others on your team, your mentor and maybe your investors. It can help you determine gaps in what your team needs to succeed and how you handle different challenges that may arise.

You can find it here.

Two tools that will help you work through your business are The Bucket Exercise and the Get Stuff Done Exercise.

The Bucket Exercise

There are four buckets of energy: Mental, Emotional, Spiritual and Physical. There are activities in our lives that drain and fill our buckets. If any one of our buckets is empty, we cannot help or give to others because we have nothing left to give. We feel drained and cannot function to the best of our ability.

Now take some time and list out what fills and what drains each of those buckets for you. There will likely be things listed in more than one bucket. For example, my kids can fill each of my buckets, but they can also drain them.

Once you have a thorough list, review the items and see the patterns. What do you notice? Are there things in your life that constantly drain your buckets? Are there not enough items to fill them? What might you change? The Blueprint Your Life exercise after this will help.

One last thing. Once you have the list of items, people or events that fill and drain your buckets, pick a few that will quickly fill each of your buckets. What is one thing that, when you do it, it will fill your bucket in less than two minutes? For me, a call to Melissa – my wife – will do it. Those quick fills will come in handy when your buckets are low.

Get Stuff Done

As entrepreneurs, we need to focus on the work at hand and block out all distractions.

This is a model for focusing our view, working on what is most important, helping make decisions, and ultimately getting more done.

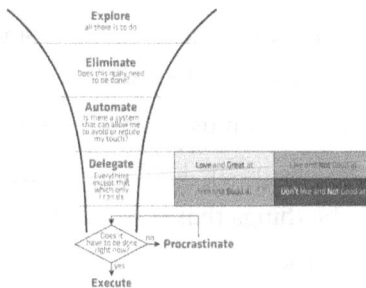

Explore

Today, there are a million messages and options available to us. I find it important to be able to see everything, to be tuned in to what is going on out there. I read hundreds of books, not to get every detail but to get the multitude of views and ideas that are discussed. I describe it as running through the trees. I don't stop and study each tree, I just run with different trees flying by me all the time. As I go, I notice patterns. When a few trees all start to show the same marks or similarities, I will stop and take a closer look at those trees to discover why that pattern has been revealed. So, that's how I explore: I look at a lot of things quickly, see patterns, and then narrow my focus.

Eliminate

In order to focus, we need to Eliminate what is not important to us or, at least, not at this time. I can't listen to every Podcast, so I choose which ones have the greatest impact. I have several friends who listen to podcasts, so I hear which episodes they recommend and listen to them. Another regular practice for me is unsubscribing from newsletters I get in my email. Inevitably, the list grows as I sign up for free items of interest or get excited about someone who is doing something innovative. Then, after a few automated emails, I start to question if each one is worth my time. It must be very high value for me to keep it. It must help to shape my focus.

Think about the things that you can eliminate, things that do not sharpen your focus.

Automate

As our focus narrows, Automation can be our friend. There are tools like RSS feeds that put the blogs you want into your inbox. Email rules are a form of automation as are email drip campaigns out to your tribe. Routine is another form of automation. When we get into a routine, it eliminates a lot of decisions and allows us to fly on autopilot, which is very efficient.

This is the reason why Steve Jobs, when he was alive, and Mark Zuckerberg always wear the same thing. Their dressing decisions are automated.

Think about areas of your life – whether tech or every day routines – that could be automated.

Delegate

Automating can apply to delegating, too. It is good to ask the question, "Does it have to be me who does this?" Many tasks might better be done by someone else. As an early entrepreneur, you need to do much of the work yourself. However, there is probably more that you can delegate than you think. Do you need to mow the lawn? Might there be a neighbourhood kid, or maybe your kid, who can?

The answer to this question is sometimes suggested by asking, "What is my time worth?" If your projects are big, your time, even if you don't pay yourself, is valuable. Ask questions about all the responsibilities or activities you have.

The only real areas you should focus on are ones you love and are great at. Everything else – especially those you don't like and are not good at – should be delegated. The figure above shows a decision matrix for delegation that we will dig into more in Step 07. In Step 05 we will talk about how you can engage others to help you, with less cost than you expect.

Keep thinking about the things that you can delegate.

Procrastinate

After you eliminated, automated, and delegated, you will probably still have a big to-do list. Now, Procrastinate. That doesn't make sense at first. However, consider how many decisions you might have made that, in hindsight, were hasty. I'm all for being decisive but taking time to make a great decision is even better. When the "change oil" light comes on in your car, you don't cancel all your appointments and drive directly to the mechanic. You book an appointment to go next Tuesday. If you are likely to forget about something, write it down (or add it to your phone) and let it come up again later.

In his famous book Getting Things Done, David Allen discusses how our minds cannot distinguish between a to-do that is due today or one due in a month. Our brain sees them both as undone, adding stress. I am happy to report I have an empty head. When something needs to get done, I add it to my reminders on my iPhone. Later, I go through them, add due dates, and assign them to a specific category list, or just do them.

Review the to-do list regularly and, when it's time for that item to be completed, do it without hesitation - execute. At that point, do not procrastinate. Leave the rest alone.

Now that you have a growing to-do list, let's go through your list and Get Stuff Done!

End of day planning

Starting today, at the end of the day when everything you are working to accomplish is fresh in your mind, take five to fifteen minutes to create your to-do list for tomorrow morning. This is the best time because you are right in the thick of it all. Your brain is working on identifying next steps already and knowing how all the work fits in to bring it to completion. This activity also helps you to have closure to the day. It will help you avoid taking the stress and left-undone items home.

The next morning, take your list and add anything else that might have reared its ugly head over the last twelve (or – ahem – four) hours. Once you have a complete list, read it through once and for the items that must get done today, label them "A". Label "B" to those items that can wait until tomorrow (Procrastination in effect) and a "C" to everything else.

Re-sort your list into the A, B, C items and, for each "A", prioritize them using A1, A2, A3 etc. as far as priority goes. I would use importance rather than urgent as a refining tool. You will know what needs to get done when.

Now you should have a list that is ordered from A1 to B's to open C's. Start at A1 and compete against yourself to get it done as fast as possible. If you come to a roadblock in needing someone else's help or something you don't have, write a note beside the item as to what is needed and put it aside. Then get to work on the next item.

55|5

The final piece to this is how to actually focus on the work at hand. I refined this idea based off the Pomodoro method detailed in the book of the same title, I use a 55 | 5 methodology instead. Sit down in your favourite workspace, turn off all distractions: Phone on airplane-mode, email and web closed, close your door, and set a timer for 55 minutes. Focus your efforts – music if you like – until the timer goes off. Once the timer goes off, take a 5-minute break. Get up, walk around, have a drink of water and, I suggest not opening any email or texts yet. Jump back into another cycle of 55 minutes followed by a 5-minute break. At this point, you could take a longer break and check in on email or other fires. Come back in the afternoon and do it all over again. Doing this cycle four times in a day may make you feel the most productive you have ever been.

The key to much of this productivity is getting others to bend to your needs rather than letting your day be shaped by others. Maybe you have heard it said that your email inbox is a big list of everyone else's attempts at getting you to do their to-dos.

If you are checking your email only a couple times a day at a specific time, you will find the expectations from your recipients begin to change. They start to realize you will get back to them at a specific time and won't bug you before that.

Once you get in the habit – and thereby getting everyone else to fall into your pace, you will get more and more accomplished each day working towards your goals.

***

Now onto the big part of this Step.

Blueprint Your Life

The reason we start with this step rather than jumping right into building the business, is because if the entrepreneur's head is in a good place, the business is easier to manage. It is also more fun for the entrepreneur.

This document is broken into several parts.

It starts by setting a date ten years in the future. Yeah, it makes me feel old, too. Just run with it. You can start with five years if it seems impossible to think ten years out. When you get there, you can look back and say "wow, I was so young and foolish then".

Many of these practices work under the understanding that the clearer the picture of your future is, the more likely you are to envision it – and take the necessary steps towards it. Even on a subconscious level, your brain will work to help you get there.

"Most people spend more time planning a one-week vacation than they do planning their life."
-- Michael Hyatt

If nothing else, these outcomes will allow you to have a filter through which you can identify practices or activities that will add to or subtract from you achieving your goals.

What is important to you?

Outcomes
While difficult for some, this little exercise is really helpful to paint a picture of the future.

Imagine you are able to attend your own funeral, as you

hear them speak about you, what do you want the people there to say about you? What do you want them to thank you for?

If you can look back at your life, it will likely be more about the people you affected than what you achieved.

I suggest the people you focus on are those closest to you and those you interact with regularly.

What do you want your God to say about you? (If you prefer to substitute the universe for God, that's fine. Just don't lose the integrity of the power of this thought.) This is, to me, the most important one. If you are dead, you are probably standing face to face now. It would be a good thing to have thought more about this situation before it is thrust upon you and now unable to be changed.

Mind you, at the point of your funeral, you can't change much anyway with any of the relationships.

This is exactly why we are trying to look at this situation. So we can change it – starting today.

The other relationships I suggest you focus on are your spouse, your dependents, your friends and those around you. These could be coworkers, fellow students, people from church or anyone that you interact with. If you really want to have some fun in your impact, think about the people who drive around you or those who serve you at the coffee shop. What do you want these people to say about you?

You may have more peer circles you want to include but I would encourage you to keep it tight. These few groups are more than enough.

Let's look at each group in a little more detail.

What do you want God to say about you? Maybe the spiritual side isn't for you. Consider if you could meet the person with the highest set of values you could imagine. What would you want them to say about you? I would hope to hear "great work! You did an excellent job with the talents and abilities you were given. You made a difference in the world and made it better. You helped others be better too."

What do you want your spouse to say about you? If you are not married, who is the most significant relationship you have? What do you hope they would say about you? Or, maybe a future spouse.

What will your children or the people who look up to you or who rely on you say about you?

And your friends? What will they say about you? What impression do you want them to have? What difference do you want to make in their lives? This is a good place to ask what you want to be thanked for.

Finally, those that you bump into. Clients, associates, workmates, the world in general. What will they say about you? What do you want them to say about you?

Remember that scene in The Lego Movie when people who Emmett bumped into regularly were being interviewed about him and couldn't say anything extraordinary about him? We don't want that in our life. What impression will we leave?

All of this may be very different than what you are doing today. That is okay. It is kind of the point. Few of us are ever operating with a mindset for the distant future.

I hate to be the bearer of bad news but one day we will all die. Bronnie Ware has a book where she summarized "The

Top Five Regrets of the Dying". These are just a few examples of what we already know: we want to have a life we love and a life of impact. The trick is setting our life up now to not have these regrets and be able to look back on our life fondly. That and have those who remember us also do it fondly.

The 7Fs

For a while, I was working full time, running a business full time, and we had three young kids. I would try to be home for dinner with the family, and each kid would take turns jumping from the top of the half stairs into my arms. However, my life was out of balance. I was working a lot and burning out and, most importantly, I was burning my wife out.

It looked as though I was a good father and husband. But I was not. I was out the door early, golfing and working, arriving home for dinner most days, then working all evening on the business and again on weekends. Because I wasn't communicating (maybe actually hearing) well with Melissa, I almost lost everything.

I'm grateful for the courage she had to say something and for the humility I had to shut up and listen. We were blessed to have a nanny after a while, but what I needed to do was get a better handle on what was really important. I believe it is a fallacy that you can have a work/life balance. They are not on either side of a set of scales. They are completely integrated, and you cannot really have one without the other.

Although no amount of planning and dreaming while sitting

on your couch eating bonbons will get you to your destination, having a clear picture of it and working with all your heart to get there will help immensely. If you take all of the areas of your life and reduce them to the essential elements, you end up with the 7Fs: Faith, Family, Friends, Fun, your Field, Fitness, and Finances.

Faith

This may refer to your personal faith or your values. How strongly connected are you personally to a higher power or purpose? Are you plugged into a community around it? Do you share about it with others?

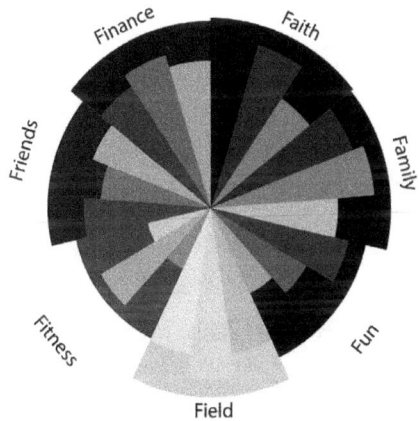

Field

Family

This includes you and your spouse or partner, if you have one, and your dependents, which could include a pet. Consider those closest to you. How do you refer to them? More importantly, how do you rate your relationship with them? What about the quality and quantity of that time?

Fun

These are the non-work life activities you are doing, and the enjoyment you are getting from them. You can have great activities and not enjoy them or have mediocre activities and really enjoy them. It is also good to be trying new activities.

Field

What is your area of specialty? You can consider a job or your schooling or your business. It could also be measured as a side hustle. As well, we should always be growing so how would you score yourself in areas of personal development? An important aspect of this is how well it provides for you, both from a revenue perspective as well as an emotional level.

Fitness

I like to focus on Exercise and Nutrition. You can work out all you want and if you continue to eat poorly, more muscle won't make you less fat. Exercise is great for keeping the blood flowing and building muscle. The battle of the physique, however, is won in the kitchen. The third vital part of Fitness is rest or sleep. Measure how you feel about your sleep.

Friends

How would you rate the quality and quantity of your relationships outside your family? Are they helping you or hurting you? I am not suggesting you need more friends by quantity. It is more: Do you feel that you have the right quantity? As an introvert, I have always been fine with one close friend. The other side of friendships: How are you serving them? Do you give to the relationships as well as enjoy them?

Finances

We must manage our finances well. This is something many of the idea-generating entrepreneurs I know generally are not good at. It is easy to manage finances when you have a lot, but remember, similar to Paul Harvey's insight:

> The three areas we measure here are your current level of debt, the level of work you are putting in to get out
>
> "If your outgo exceeds your income, your updeep will be your downfall."

of debt, and how much of a gap between your income and expenditures – breathing room.

***

Now, look at each of the 7Fs and create an ideal picture in ten years for each. Take into consideration the different elements (spokes) within each F as well. For example, in Family, there is spouse, dependents, and time. When you create your ten year vision for your Family, it will likely include what it will look like with both your spouse and kids and the quality of family time.

Write it as if you could not fail. We can get caught up in all the what-ifs and that-will-never-happens and we miss the opportunity to dream a little. Push yourself to do this with an optimistic view.

Your Why

Life can get very difficult at times. Business can push you to the brink. The thing that keeps us going is the outcome we want, whether it is the six-pack abs or the Lamborghini on the wall. Hopefully, it is something much bigger, a higher purpose, a calling. The difference you want to make in the world is your Why.

Take some time and think about, and write down, your big Why.

Your Ideal Week

If you are going to work on your life, you need to create time for these elements in your schedule. How do you fit something new into an already packed life? Like you would a jammed suitcase: Open it up, examine what is really needed and get rid of what is not as important.

The form for this exercise is a blank calendar. I suggest colour coordinating your schedule, so you can quickly see where your time is being spent. Here are my colours and their meaning:

Mellow Yellow

Personal time. Put this in first. Most entrepreneurs don't spend enough time relaxing. When working a muscle, it needs time to recover after times of stress. We are no different. Downtime helps us rejuvenate. Book this in first to make sure you get some. I have added another colour (purple) here for Family or my wife. This is also a vital part of things for my overall health.

Red Tape

Administration time. Nothing is more of a time-suck than spending a month entering all your expenses and receipts in a mad rush at tax time. Rather, take an hour each week to do some administration. Update your books, enter receipts, make those Accounts Payable phone calls you need to make. All you need is an hour or two, but make sure it is in your calendar.

Blue Sky

Strategic Planning. You need to climb a tree to look around

once in a while so you don't end up going around in circles through the forest of life. At the start of the year, I put in quarterly retreat times to review this calendar and my life blueprint. I also keep a little time on Monday mornings to review the week and make sure everything that needs to get done this week is scheduled in.

Green Machine

Money making. Many entrepreneurs default to this being the first thing that goes in the calendar. While I understand why, this often means the business runs the entrepreneur. Following the order I proposed here, there will be plenty of time for money making appointments and activities. I have also distinguished between prospecting green and delivery green. That way I can tell if it is billable time or creating new business. You definitely want both.

Orange Leader

Spiritual. I have a lot of involvement in my church, but it has also been a way for me to allocate my focus times in the morning rather than just making them personal. You will have your own spiritual or value-building time.

Now to fill in the calendar.

Daniel Pink in his book *When* speaks very well on the power of understanding your own circadian rhythms to know what times you are better at cerebral versus creative thinking and when you need down time.

For me, my strategy planning times are best done on either Sunday night or Monday morning. This way, I get my head wrapped around the week before I get too far into it. I also take some time on Monday to get Admin done because the end of the week is the rush to tie up all the loose business ends – at that time I'm not thinking about admin

I also add appointments with myself to do the Administration or Delivery for my clients. Often, I have homework time. If something important AND timely comes up for that same time, I can move the homework time to another slot. However, if I fill my calendar at the whim of others, I never get my homework done. I let others book time with me through Calendly (automation in action). They can see the open spots and book according to my schedule rather than me bending to only their requests.

That sums up Step 01.

***

Congratulations. You have just accomplished something that fewer than 5% of the population ever does. This planning is the difference maker to your success.

Keep referring back to this document and update this information regularly.

Now we move into working on the business.

STEP 02 - Know Your Customers

Businesses often undertake what is called Hope Marketing. They put out a product and hope it is seen as valuable and will get adopted. Some entrepreneurs say, "I would totally buy this, so others must be willing to," or a slightly different version: "Everyone I talk to says this is a good idea."

There are many businesses that are best classified as zombies: not really alive, not really dead - and eating the brains of the entrepreneurs.

The way to avoid all of this is to go deep on your definition of the problem and provide a meaningful solution.

Think of this definition of an entrepreneur:

In the saturated market today, if your solution isn't extraordinary or incredibly unique – and

"One who facilitates consistent solutions to a well-defined problem."

marketed well – you won't be heard, you won't be seen, and your business will, at best, underperform, at worst, fail completely.

Quite simply, you need to really understand the person you are creating the solution for. Even when your solution is directed at an enterprise or corporation rather than a consumer, you will be selling directly to someone who has a problem and needs a solution for their team, their company, their brand.

Since you are selling to a person, you can talk to that person and get details on the problem they are having rather than assuming you know what the problem really is. The more people you ask, the more you understand the nuances of the problem.

There may be a fear that comes with talking to prospects.

Something along the lines of "if I talk to that person, if I can even get to one of them, they will trash the idea and I'm dead in the water" or "if I talk with other people about this problem before I have a solution, someone might steal my idea."

These are both legitimate concerns. Consider this, however: if your proposed solution is shot down early by several people, you either don't have a good solution, or you have a good solution that needs more work. Now you have a number of new ideas to make it better and the best part, you now have made a number of contacts that might be your early adopters.

As for the second concern, your solution may be too valuable not to talk about. I have found that most people are not out to steal ideas. Usually I am more ambitious and have more momentum than someone else taking my idea and trying to make it their own. Further, I believe the private ownership of Intellectual Property (IP) is becoming less important. We are moving more to a collaborative society. When someone thinks you have a great idea, they are more than likely willing to throw their hat in the ring with you rather than try to compete against you.

Step 02 has a few different areas: What is the problem? Who is the problem being solved for? What is the cost of the problem? How can you create a pitch to start talking about it with others? And how does the customer travel through the introduction and buying experience?

There are also two more tools that help in this process: The Value Curve Analysis and the Empathy Map.

Empathy Map

In entrepreneurial circles, it is common to hear conversations about WIIFM – What's In It For Me? The investors want to know this, the customers want to know this, you want to know this, and so does your family.

This exercise will help you get into the mind of the customer and understand What's In It For Them?

In the centre is your target audience. Describe them in as much detail as you can. Then, from their perspective, fill in each of the rest of the areas. What do they think and feel? What are they wrestling with? What is their internal battle?

Next, what do they hear? What are their friends saying? What is the news saying? What is part of their culture they hear from their parents, friends, kids, peer groups?

What do they see? What are they seeing on TV, on YouTube, on the Internet in general? What are they watching? Where are they watching it? What is their field of vision?

From their perspective, what do they say and do? What are they experiencing? What language, of words, phraseology and messages do they speak. What do they do with their lives? Where are they? Where do they go and hang out?

What pain are they trying to avoid and what gain are they trying to achieve? How does it manifest itself? What does it feel like? What does it look or sound like? How does it affect them?

The clearer you are about each of these areas, the more likely you will parallel your solution to the problem the hero is experiencing.

Of course, the best way to get this information is to go and ask. Go talk to prospective clients and ask a ton of questions. Most people are happy to be listened to... especially if you are going to work to create a solution for them.

Set up some time with client prospects and even frame the meetings as information gathering. You could try something like this:

"We are in the process of building a solution to this problem and we believe you are experiencing elements of that problem. Might we get thirty minutes together to discuss how it affects you and how we might customize a solution that works for you? Please understand this is not a sales meeting. We are not at that stage and merely gathering information from valued people experiencing this problem."

Here is a little phrase to remember when you face some difficulties:

The more you talk to **"When in doubt, talk it out."** your clients and prospects, the better you understand them and their problem. This, when acted upon, will create better solutions and therefore higher revenues and better customer engagement.

Here's another tip:

"Do for one what you wish you You do not need to **could do for many."** bend to the whim of **-- Andy Stanley** every client, but you can get input from them all and tailor something that works for the majority – more specifically, your target audience.

It is better to have a small audience of raging fans than it is to have a massive audience of mediocre ones.

When you make a difference for even one client, you still make a difference. News of this success will also get around and build your brand and reputation. Don't be concerned with thinking everyone will now demand this extra treatment. Treat each situation with wisdom and integrity.

Value Curve

The book Blue Ocean Strategy talks about building a brand away from the "red ocean" where all the competition is found, and instead building in the "blue ocean" where the competition is missing something.

In order to discover where the blue ocean is, you need to look carefully. This tool will help you determine where you might zig to the competitions zag.

There are many examples of zigging when the competition zags.

Starbucks created an environment where people are welcome to sit and drink coffee all day instead of popping in to buy a coffee and leave.

iTunes saw the rise of digital music and created the sale of the file/song rather than the album.

Canon created colour copiers for home and for secretaries seeing that people wanted individual copiers on their desk.

Tesla created high performance electric cars with no stores. The whole process is fan based.

A note about positioning a business: It is difficult when an entrepreneur feels like they are pigeon-holed – to be told they are just like so-and-so. However, against a backdrop of thousands of messages a day, we need to be able to categorize people and businesses quickly.

When you say, "We're the YouTube of the medical industry," a prospective client can give a sigh of relief and say, "Oh, that makes sense," rather than, "What is it you do again?" When you state your model as, "We're the x of the y," your hearers will be better able to understand.

When it comes to a new offering, being pigeonholed is actually a good thing.

However, you just need to be clear on what your difference is.

Define the Problem

Now we get into the heart of this Step. The outcome of this Step is to understand your market, your specific buyer, and your solution.

The object here is to really empathize with the buyer and flesh out everything you can about the problem. Stretch the boundaries to why the problem is happening, how much it costs, who experiences it, and how it makes them feel. Then you can start discovering who else is working on solutions or in similar areas.

You will want to go deeper on the costs of the problem. How much does this problem cost the target client each day, week, month, year? How much do the current "solutions" that don't work cost?

Can you be sure the client is willing to pay for the problem? How can you tell?

I have found that when entrepreneurs do surveys and have conversations with prospects, they will ask something like, "How much are you willing to pay for something like this?" The answers will get you into a ballpark of the right answer, but until someone opens their wallet, there is no confirmation that someone will pay that.

A better gauge on this is called the Minimum Viable Product (MVP). What is the quick and messy, full of bugs, duct taped together, barely working product that you can present to see if there is some interest? Even with all the flaws, something in someone's hands will generate an excellent indicator of interest.

Nick Swinmurn took pictures of shoes in a mall to test if there was an interest in people buying shoes online without trying them on first and posted them online to see how people would react. They weren't even his company's shoes. People liked it and Zappos was born.

The first version of the iPad (the Newton) was carved out of wood.

One local company developed a software product for contractor businesses. Just when the client was about to sign up, they said, "We're really happy you like it. Can we give it to you at a discount for the next six months and follow you around everywhere getting your feedback?" They signed up six beta clients and now have a successful, well-refined product for their business.

The point is, get a concept of your idea into the hands of

people, ask a ton of questions about it, and keep refining until it has a wow factor.

Now try to wrap everything into a mission or purpose statement.

Remember, our definition of Mission: who you serve and how you serve them. Might you put one or two sentences together that state this clearly?

Here is mine for *The Entrepreneur Roadmap*: "We help entrepreneurs avoid needless failure."

A Social Enterprise I operate uses this: "We're ending poverty through well-executed entrepreneurship and micro-loans."

Pitching Pause

Let's talk about pitching

What is the point of all this talk we hear about short statements and elevator pitches?

This is important because we are always pitching. We pitch to get investment, we pitch to customers to buy our product, we pitch to vendors to work with us, we pitch to current and prospective employees, we pitch to our friends as well talk about what we do, we pitch at networking events, and we even need to pitch to our spouse and kids to justify the time and resources we spend on our business.

Therefore, getting our pitch right is really important.

Remember,

"A confused mind says 'NO.'"

If you can get your idea down to a succinct few sentences, even one sentence that you can explain to a ten-year-old and have them understand it, you have a winning pitch.

Most pitches and explanations are jargony, too long, uninteresting, and not engaging, the exact opposite of what you want and need for your business.

Here is my framework for a three-sentence pitch.

1. You know how...
2. We solve that by...
3. Imagine if...

The first sentence is about getting buy-in on the problem you are solving. You want to state the problem in a way that everyone will get it. If you say it right, the person you are talking to will nod.

You know how ...

- You know how Facebook always seems to be spying on you...
- You know how everyone has an idea for a business and very few know how to build a business around that idea...
- You know how drywall is heavy and causes workplace injuries...

This sentence should illuminate the problem for them.

Now they will be listening for your solution.

We solve that by...

- We solve that by creating a simple software app that protects you from Facebook's prying eyes.
- We have solved that by creating a simple roadmap for entrepreneurs to follow at their own pace.

- We have solved that by creating an innovative lightweight drywall...

The way I refer to this part also becomes the basis for a one-sentence pitch – or answer to "what do you do?" We do WHAT, for WHO, HOW. Answer that for the second sentence.

At this point, the engaged person might be itching to ask you more questions. One more sentence to go.

Imagine if...

This actually works as a command. It will encourage your listener to start imaging the possibilities.

- Imagine if you could enjoy Facebook without having to worry that the world will know too much about you.
- Imagine if we could eliminate needless failure for entrepreneurs.
- Imagine if we could change the face of the drywall market by allowing anyone to be able to install it.

This kind of a pitch will completely open up the conversation with your listener. Now they are engaged and understand what you are doing. They might not need the solution themselves, but they will likely know someone who could benefit and might offer to make an introduction.

If nothing else, they will remember you and where to categorize you in their brain.

Avoid the audience having a confused mind that says "no" and create a simple pitch that engages instead of confuses.

Customer Journey

Imagine the first sale and what will it take to get there. More importantly, what the customer experiences through the process. Write that down and keep modifying it and learning how to make it work better. Track everything. Use a spreadsheet if you must.

There needs to be a specific plan for the public to become customers. How do you get their attention? What are the different channels you use to get their attention? Once you have their attention, how and when do they convert to a prospect? When you have them as a prospect, what steps do you take them through to get them to convert to a sale? Who meets with them? What materials do they get? How do you measure the progress? How is it entered into your tracking tools?

Mature companies do this and follow it with engineering-like discipline. Entrepreneurs are famous for winging it and wondering why they don't get the revenues they want. This is a hard practice to get right in the early days as you just want to make a sale and are excited by anyone who wants to buy something. I'll give you that. Once you have one sale, sit down and think about what it took to make it happen. A half-baked sales process is better than no sales process. Ask the questions above after each sale.

Remember the lemniscate of the Entrepreneur Roadmap. Doing it once will get you started. You need to keep going back and getting better at each part.

STEP 03 – Manage Your Money

You may have the best idea in the world. However, if it is unable to make money, it becomes a very expensive hobby. If customers want to use your product or service but it is priced out of a reasonable range, they won't buy it.

That being said, some businesses take a while to start making money. That is fine. However, it needs to be intentional.

You also should know how much money your solution makes, when it will make money, how it makes money, when the money comes in, where the money is spent, who is spending it, and then keep important measures of business success at your fingertips.

In order to get a good handle on the finance side of your business, there are a number of terms you will need to know. They are Cost Of Good Sold (COGS), Cost of Acquisition, Budget, Breakeven, Cash Flow, Cash Cycles, Debt, Investors, Savings, Personal Finance, and Key metrics. Let's look deeper into each one. Investopedia.com (started and sold by a local entrepreneur friend) is a great resource for all financial terms.

COGS: Cost Of Goods Sold. Another term is Cost of Revenue, which can apply to service-based companies. Consider what it costs to make your solution. There are raw materials to put together, there is the act of manufacturing your product, there is labour, there is shipping. What does it cost to get your product from idea to the point it is ready to sell? For a service, there are the time and resources to create and design the service experience.

Cost of Acquisition: What it costs to win a client. What marketing tools do you use to attract someone to your front door, your webpage, or your conversion tool? What materials do they get? Think of ebooks, brochures, samples. What do you do to help them become a paying customer? Are there meetings, coffees, golf games, more materials, presentations, samples? Can you get to a specific ROI for every dollar spent on marketing?

Budget: Determining your monthly revenue and income. I recommend a lot of phone calls, calling utilities, internet providers, landlords, etc. to get accurate numbers. Talk to companies like BusinessLink (in Canada) who can help you get numbers for all sorts of things. They can do marketing research as well.

Most entrepreneurs underestimate costs, especially of employees. For starters, I recommend paying yourself, but not excessively. After all, how long will you keep at something this challenging if you're not getting paid? Remember there is a part that is paid to the government on an employee's behalf as well. This is called "burden" and can be around 8% of the employee's salary, more if you include benefits.

Cash Flow: My entrepreneur friend Blaine Bertch wrote a book called Pandemic Cash Flow in which he shows that 30% of businesses fail due to cash flow problems but 70% of those businesses were profitable when they died. Let that sink in.

If your budget shows incomes and expenses, then cash flow is when everything happens. What days of the month does money come in and monies go out? Cash flow is king. Rather than thinking "revenue - expenses = profit" start thinking "revenue - profit = expenses." Because we tend to find a way to spend the money we have, we will have nothing left for profit. Take profit out first and put it away. The money left is what you have to work with. Once you set target averages for everything, you can work within those boundaries to put money away and pay bills, taxes and everything else your business needs... including owner's salary.

Cash Cycle: the time it takes between paying the costs to make your solution and getting paid for delivering your solution to the client. A positive cash cycle means you get paid in advance of delivering the solution. Most products work this way. We expect to pay for products before we use them. A negative cash cycle means you are delivering your solution, and paying expenses before you get paid. This sometimes is the time it takes to do the work; plus the time it takes for your clients to get around to paying your bill. That could be Net 30 or Net 180. That's a long time to be without cash.

The problem – obvious above – with a negative cash flow is you are out of pocket until you get paid. The problem with positive cash flow is usually only in recording it. If it takes you four months to finish the solution, even though you are collecting money up front, you need to spread that income across the whole delivery time– according to Generally Accepted Accounting Practices (GAAP).

Breakeven: The inflection point where your revenues yield a profit over expenses. Some businesses can do this from day one. Others take years to get to this point. Knowing this point and the cost of getting there is vital to the business. Once you know these elements, you need to figure out what you will do to supplement the revenues in order to make expenses? This can be done through investors, loans: from outside or inside, or other creative ways. Keep in mind: things often take three times as long and cost twice as much as you expect.

Debt: I don't like debt. While not as expensive as giving a portion of your business away to investors via equity, debt still costs money. It would be important to run scenarios to determine if debt is the best way to go rather than being lean and growing organically. I recognize that sometimes you need to get ahead of the curve and debt is a viable answer to that. What is the cost of borrowing? What is the advantage of borrowing? What are the creative alternatives?

Investors: They range from what some call Friends, Family and Fools: these are inexperienced investors who give you money because they love you or love your idea. As much as they are hoping for a great return and some magic, they are mostly giving you money without the analytics to understand if it is a good idea.

The next class of investors might be Angels. These are usually experienced businesspeople who have made money and want to help entrepreneurs get to the next level and make a return on the way. Amounts might range from $5000 to under $100,000 – rarely higher.

The next level opens a world of definitions: the Venture Capital market. We see them on the Shark Tank and Dragon's Den. Where the Friends, Family and Fools may do little to no due diligence and Angels will do quite a bit more, VCs will do extensive analysis and due diligence to ensure their money is being allocated to the right places to have the best chance to win. They don't expect every deal to win big, but they are looking for those who can create a tenfold return or more on their investment. Angels may invest because they have a passion for the entrepreneur or industry or idea. VCs tend to be more clinical.

Be careful about finding a good fit, and don't take it personally if they say "no." There are a number of other investor groups out there.

Savings: You can't weather a storm if you don't have any resources to do so. I encourage entrepreneurs to have six to twelve months worth of expenses put away in savings.

Personal Finance: If you are not good at personal finances, it will be hard to be good at your business finances. Here's a reminder of seven important points made famous by Dave Ramsay. 1. Put $1000 in the bank for quick access in an emergency. 2. Debt snowball. List all your debts from smallest to largest and put as much as possible to them each month and snowball the amounts until they are all paid off. The only thing not in this list would be your house. 3. Fully fund your personal emergency account from the $1000 to three to six months of expenses (six to twelve months if you are an entrepreneur). 4. Put 15-25% of your income into investments for retirement. 5. Save for your children's education. 6. Pay off the house. 7. Build wealth and grow in generosity.

There is a cash flow tool available here. In Part III at the end there are a few other financial tools available as well.

Your Scorecard

Key metrics: How will you measure the health of your business? Is profit the most important number? What metrics show leading indicators of success? Consider conversions on the webpage, the number of calls made, the number of meetings attended? There should be between five and fifteen key numbers or key metrics at your fingertips. Pick a few numbers and get them weekly. After a few meetings with the leadership team, you will start discovering new numbers or better ones. Let it evolve over time until you can practically predict the future days and weeks – maybe even years – of your business. This is when you know you have it right. The numbers still may change as the business evolves.

Revenue isn't the only number, but it is an important one. If you are not selling, you will not stay in business.

Some metrics may be around the value you add to the public. What is important to them?

Sometimes the metrics are users or partnerships or reviews. The important thing is to experiment until you have numbers that really give you the ongoing story of what is important in your business. Just like a dashboard of a car showing you the important information for your journey at a glance.

Once you have the numbers you need, each team member should have a number that they know and understand that measures their success. This could be a sales target, a manufacturing target, a customer satisfaction level. Each team member deserves to know how to be successful each day. This will create a productive and enjoyable culture.

The Pivot

Let's say you get through all this and determine that your numbers, your market or your model just doesn't work. Some entrepreneurs deny what the reality says and keep persevering. Others give up to never try again. How do you know when to pivot and when to persevere?

This is where people whom you admire and allow to speak into your business come in. Remember,

"The one with the most information makes the best decisions."

The numbers above give some insight and that, along with the advice of valued people, will help you make the best decisions. Things cannot always work out perfectly no matter how much you know. Get as much information as you can and make the best decision you can at the time. Step 07 has a tool to help with this.

STEP 04 – Map out Your Plan

Working with entrepreneurs over the years, I have noticed a disconnect between their dreams or vision and the here and now. It's easy to dream and hard to put those dreams into action. This Step is all about getting traction towards your ultimate vision.

Think of your plan as if you were using a telescope and a microscope. The telescope is all about the future. However, if all you ever do is stare into the telescope, it's awfully hard not to trip over what's right in front of you.

The microscope is all about the details, what is going on today. Just as with the telescope, though, if you only look through the microscope, you can get lost in the details.

The two must work together. The microscope is key to dealing with today and the near future, and the telescope is key to know where you are trying to go.

Let's take a telescopic look at how we bridge the gap between here and there.

The Business Blueprint

There is a practical way to take those lofty visions and turn them into a to do list for today.

This is a one-page overview of the tool.

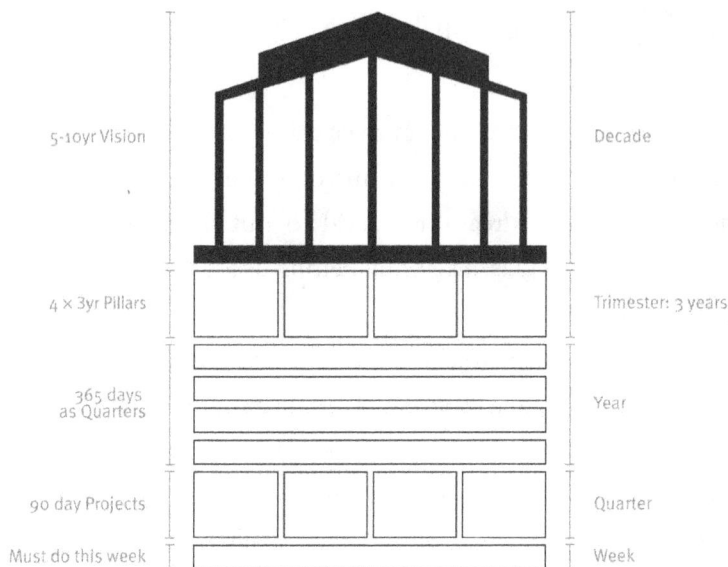

5-10yr Vision		Decade
4 × 3yr Pillars		Trimester: 3 years
365 days as Quarters		Year
90 day Projects		Quarter
Must do this week		Week

Exercise 1

First, describe your business in ten years the way you want it to look. How much revenue do you have? What is your role and level of involvement? What reputation do you have as a business? This should line up with your personal blueprint from Step 01. If your vision for your business doesn't jive with your vision for your life, you will be filled with a tension you won't like. The two will be pulling on you in different directions.

Hopefully the vision you have just created for your business is exciting and a little scary. Jim Collins in his book Built to Last uses the term

"A BHAG engages people – it reaches out and grabs them in the gut. It is tangible, energizing, highly focused. People 'get it' right away; it takes little or no explanation."
-- Jim Collins

BHAG: Big Hairy Audacious Goal.
It is a clear and compelling vision.

Exercise 2

The second exercise in the process is building a three-year foundation. Just like building a skyscraper, there is a lot of work to be done on the foundation before it can support a 50 or 150-storey building. Your business is the same. If the business will take about ten years to achieve your vision, in three years, you really need to have established that foundation.

Take some time to brainstorm possible pillars that absolutely need to be in place for the company to become your vision. There might be certain processes in place or key roles hired. Maybe specific products must be designed and ready to launch by this point. The brainstorming session is the place to get all these ideas on paper.

After the brainstorming, look at the list and pick four that absolutely must be completed in three years. Usually they are obvious. If they are not, pick the ones you believe are key. Sometimes any direction is a good direction. Also, this document should become a living one for you to review regularly so things are able to change. That said, choosing a direction and executing is an important element of being an entrepreneur.

These are the cornerstones for your business, the most important components to build your future business upon.

Exercise 3

Exercise 3 is focused on the next 365 days. Of your

cornerstones, which ones – or what parts of them – need to be completed in the next year to get you one third of the way to your three-year goal?

Think of living your life backwards, from fulfillment to initiation. Examine your completed cornerstones and consider how you got there. Ask, "What needed to be in place in order to have that cornerstone done?" Keep moving backwards in time towards today and you will have a step-by-step plan of what needs to be done.

For each of the cornerstones, repeat the process and start putting these elements into each of the four quarters of the year. You can start with the fourth quarter and keep moving back to the previous quarter. Looking at these quadrants, you should have an idea of the big items you need to tackle this year to get serious traction towards your cornerstones – and ultimately towards your vision.

Exercise 4

The fourth exercise zooms in on the upcoming quarter – your next 90 days.

Now we take this quarter and break it into three to five projects. There is a project outline tool in Step 06. Each of these projects will have:

1. A project name so you can refer to it easily.
2. Only one person responsible for it. There may be several people on the project but there can be only one person who is responsible.
3. It will have a clearly defined outcome, so everyone can tell that it is completed.

4. The timeline is always for 90 days so it will be not too big and not too small.

5. A budget if required. Is there money allotted for this project? Does it need money?

6. At least three actions to complete.

7. Finally, metrics to measure the results of the actions

These quarterly projects are different for a team than for an individual entrepreneur. For a team, each person can have a few projects. For an individual entrepreneur, well, it's all on you... choose wisely. Don't bite off more than you can chew and be careful to choose the ones that have the highest impact in moving your business forward.

Exercise 5

The last exercise is "The Must-Do" list. There are a million things to do each day in business and the list never stops growing. However, we know there is a difference between what is urgent and what is important. The Must-Do list is important.

Take each of the projects you, and each person on your team, is responsible for and determine what needs to be done this week to move each project forward. Write it down and then, simply do it. Each week. Every week.

Build in a weekly or quarterly cycle of reviewing your Business Blueprint from telescope to microscope, adjust as needed and move items into your weekly Must-Dos and then do them. Every 90 days create new projects and subsequent Must-Dos and then accomplish them.

Every day do something to move your business forward. Go

back to the productivity tool in Step 01 for how to Get Stuff Done.

There are a number of tools in Step 05 and 06 that will help you keep these projects moving. At the very least, once you have your Must-Dos, an accountability partner can help to keep your feet to the fire.

Make sure you pick someone who will do that. If your spouse lets you off the hook, well, your business may not move forward at the pace you want it to. Pick someone, like a mentor, that will check in with you or with whomever you have regular meetings, even if it's once a month. You bring your Must-Do list from each week and have the other person sign off on it.

The ideal situation is with a team. Each week, you get together and discuss your Must Dos. Simply knowing you will have to report on it each week will often be enough to get it done.

That is how you take your BHAG and work it into what you must do this week to get there.

Let's look at a couple more tools available to help.

One-Page Business Blueprint

The Lean Business Model Canvas has become a ubiquitous tool for business planning. For those who know how to use it, it is powerful.

The value of the tool is having your business model on one page to hand to people or to work through easily on an ongoing basis.

This has all the core elements for your business: Vision,

Mission, Values, Goals, Markets, Revenue sources, Customer details etc.

This is something you can have handy to refer to or revise as needed.

Business is ever-changing. New technologies come into play, new competitors come into the landscape, people, places and product lines change. Instead of a business plan that most write and shelve, this One-Page Business Blueprint (1PBB) can be a living document that is constantly used and improved to meet the changes in your business environment.

Implementation Planner

Investors – and you – want to know two things:
1. Are the numbers you state for that hockey-stick growth realistic?
2. Do you have the plan and the team to carry out the expected ROI?

This tool is designed to map out exactly what is needed for resources, finances, and projects on a quarterly basis to get you to your goal.

Down the left-hand side, the rows state four sections.
1. Administration/Finance
2. Sales and marketing
3. Product development or Manufacturing
4. Operations

Across the top, the columns are quarters.

Each quarter might have projects in each of the four

sections. Each project, as discussed earlier, has a name, responsible person, budget, outcomes and milestones.

You may have to manually total the costs of each project at the bottom. Doing this will give you a quarterly requirement financially.

Using this in conjunction with your budget and key numbers will help you know when your spending occurs and where your breakeven will appear. Of course, all things going according to plan.

***

Aside from building a team – a fundamental part of business – the tools we covered in this section will help you build a viable business and give you the best chance of success.

PART II – IMPROVE

Review

Up until now, much of the work done on your business might have been done on your own. While the work on all the Steps before this can be shared, from this point forward, we will grow in complexity and, likely, the team.

Remember, The Entrepreneur Roadmap is designed as a lemniscate. As you cycle around and deepen your understanding in each area, you cross right through Step 04 each time. This is one of the most important parts of the whole model.

It is important to make this a part of your regular planning routine. Whether it is weekly, monthly or quarterly, review this and refine it. Live and breathe it.

Okay, let's start building a team.

STEP 05 – Build Your Team

While getting a great team together is vital for success, it is not an easy task.

You must have a few key roles

First, you should have someone who can create the big vision for the company. This is the dreamer and big picture person – the Steve Jobs. Then you need someone who gets stuff done. This is the implementer, often different than the dreamer because they have a drive to make things happen – the Tim Cook. You also need someone needs to be good at financials and managing the money, someone for sales and marketing, someone who is good at culture and hiring, a technology specialist to keep everything running, someone with industry experience, and finally, ideally, a mentor – someone who has the experience to help the leadership of the team navigate the complexities of business.

Of course, an experienced team is important.

However, experience is one thing; how well everyone functions together is THE difference maker. A diverse, experienced team that works well together is a powerhouse.

Within our Accelerator, we use the Leadership Matrix evaluation tool to review the make-up and strength of the leadership team. You can find it here to work through.

Building Culture

How do you build the culture you need for success?

You need the right team – the right fit. Fit trumps everything. Fit also changes as the company changes. Every new person you hire creates a new culture.

First rule: Don't hire out of convenience.

This is a mistake most entrepreneurs make over and over. Hiring can be tough, I know. It's hard to find good people, and there is real pain associated with having an empty spot on your team when you have a lot to get done. However, it is even more painful having a full team that isn't doing what it's supposed to be doing.

The 4Cs

There are a million tests you can do to evaluate your team.

I like to use the 4Cs: Character, Competency, Chemistry and Capacity.

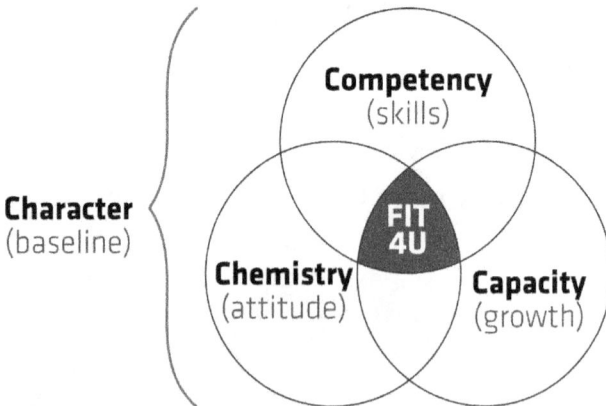

Character is all about who the person is. Are they friendly, relatable, humorous, honest, on-time?

Competency is where most entrepreneurs – and most companies for that matter – focus. Can they do the job? I like to ask "should they do the job?" You can train for skills; you can't do much to modify the other three Cs. However, you still want to be sure someone has the competency to do the job. Competency can be proven through auditions.

Chemistry. This deals with a person's fit on the team, with the culture of the team, the group, and the company.

Chemistry is how well an employee understands and agrees with the direction of the vision for the company. Chemistry is holding to the same values as the company. Chemistry is about being aligned with how to deliver to the customer, the view of the customer, with the view of the team. Chemistry is also about behaving in a way that people around them approve, applaud and admire.

Capacity has three aspects.

1. Does the candidate have the capacity to do the job when needed? A part-time person for a full-time job is a capacity issue. A day-shift person for a night-shift role is a capacity issue.

2. Another side is the ability to grow with the role as the company or role grows. If you need someone who can learn to adapt and they are not able, it is a capacity issue.

3. Finally, do they have the capacity to understand the role? Can they wrap their head around all that is needed and expected of them?

When these 4Cs are understood and questioned for each role and each person, you will have a better dynamic for hiring.

The tool I use for this is called The People Fit tool. This will help you objectively determine the fit of each team member and anyone new you will bring on to your team. Try it out here:

Fixing Culture

Since we throw the word around a lot, let's define culture.

Every company has a culture. Sometimes, it's like water to a fish. It is there and you survive in it regardless of what it's like. You may not recognise it as a defined culture. It just is.

A great way to test your culture is look around and question: Who gets rewarded for what behaviours. Who gets promoted? Who gets the bonuses? Why did they get the promotion? Why did that person get chosen over someone else? What do the team members say about who gets rewarded for what? Sometimes this is intentional, sometimes it is not. It is, however, the culture you have.

Can employees have a real conversation with you about what they see? Are they told they are delusional or "that's just the way it is" Do you ask and seek honest answers from employees?

The answers to these questions go a long way to defining culture.

If you want to hear the truth, go ask your favourite employees that quit why they quit. It will likely illuminate the bad parts of your culture.

If you have good honest communication, through practices

like Core 4 meetings, daily check-ins, weekly team meetings, quarterly offsite activities, and ad hoc strategy meetings, you will see timely things about your culture that need to be addressed. Start addressing them.

Releasing

This is a good a time to talk about firing. I like to call it releasing. For starters, it is important to understand that someone who might not be performing well in your company may end up being great in another company.

Someone may thrive in one environment and consider another one toxic.

In a previous role as a recruiter, leaders would call me in and state, "I want the most talented person for this role." I'd look around at their team and say (much more politely) "If I bring a thoroughbred into this den of donkeys, they will bounce right back out the door." High performers want to be around other high performers.

Now, take into consideration that high performance means different things to different people.

This is why culture is so complex. You should not – and could not – have the same culture as the company beside you. Stop trying to be Google. Be the best you.

So, just because someone doesn't fit in with your team, does not mean they won't fit in better somewhere else. Looking at firing as releasing may help make it a little easier.

How do we release someone respectfully?

Have them into a meeting. Likely, they will know why they're there. If they don't, let them know. Clear is kind, unclear is unkind. Once you are on the same page that performance – or something – needs to change, you can ask a question. "What can you do to make this change?" Let them share and dig for clarity and understanding. Keep asking until they listed everything or run out of ideas. Share a few of your own if there is something missing.

Once that is exhausted, ask the next question: "How long will it take to make this change?" Help them be realistic on this. Make sure it is a reasonable amount of time.

Last question: "What do you need from me to ensure this happens?" Again, dig for clarity and understanding. Write everything out on a document and both sign off on it.

Finally, produce what they need from you immediately. Now they have no excuse not to do what is needed other than their own integrity. They will either step up and change what is needed or walk themselves out the door.

At your next quarterly meetings (or sooner) with your leadership team, take a day and work through these core cultural elements.

Patrick Lencioni puts up six questions in his book *The Advantage* that are a good starting point.

1. Why do we exist? (mission)
2. How do we behave? (values)
3. What do we do? (mission again)
4. How will we succeed? (goals)
5. What is important right now? (goals)
6. Who must do what? (goals)

Armed with the answers to these questions, you can put the elements into place to carry out a culture shift. Then you should over-communicate them through your organization every chance you get.

Believe it or not, you will get sick of hearing this speech far before your team will. Your team wants to be a part of something great. If companies looked at their employees as volunteers instead, they might be better off. After all, employees don't stick around just because you pay them. A paycheque is not a retention strategy. If they are only there for the paycheque, you likely have employees who are disengaged and who make you feel like you are pushing string to get them motivated. Volunteers, by contrast, love to be a part of a cause and give up their free time to do so. That same process applies to employees. Get them rallied around Lencioni's six questions, and you are off to a great start.

One further lesson about this. When you get a strong culture started, it becomes a magnet. It attracts more like-minded people and it deters the rest. A strong culture is repulsive to the wrong people and magnetic to the right ones.

> "Culture eats Strategy for breakfast."
> --Peter Drucker

Hiring

Let's talk about good hiring practices.

In order to achieve successful hiring, your team should discuss each of the following elements, and a process should be established. The process is put in place to ensure no one sidesteps just because you

feel "this guy is different." You need to trust the process enough that your best prospects will be discovered and those you don't want will be discouraged by going through it.

The following diagram is something I have worked on over the years as I've gone about hiring.

Don't forget the WHY

Great hiring starts by asking ourselves, "Why?"

Many times, the answer to that question seems to be, "Because I need someone to do this or that." Instead, we should slow down and look at the big picture, or at least get a deeper clarification.

Here are some questions to ask yourself:

- What is missing in our current talent pool?
- What is not getting done?

- What role will be most important in the next six months, in the next year?
- Do we need someone temporary or permanent?
- How do we better meet our clients' needs?
- Who is most overwhelmed in their current role? Why?
- How might we best redistribute the workload to delay hiring?
- Do we have the finances to sustain such a role?

role definition

Tell me about the ROLE

Now that you know why you are hiring, put down some specifics about the role itself.

What are the key responsibility areas (KRA) for this role? Can you describe in a sentence or two the area in which you want a person to succeed?

There are two major reasons for this:

1. When the role is distilled like this, you have given enough thought to what truly needs to get done. It is like you have the puzzle pieces all put together and there is one well-defined piece missing. Your new hire will be that piece.

2. When the role is defined this well, the person taking on the role will know what the "win" is each day they come to work. Team members with a hundred items in their role description are unsure of where they make the most impact. They lack focus and therefore, lack productivity. A well-defined role also makes it easier to identify the next element.

WHO?

WHO is the ideal person?

When the Body Shop comes out with a new product, they dig into so many demographics and psychographics that they literally design a cardboard cutout of the perfect client. It has the brands they wear, what they might look like and many of the characteristics of their ideal patron. So much so, that when this person walks through the door, staff would be able to identify them immediately. This is referred to as an avatar.

Our hiring should be the same. Consider it Employee Marketing. When the ideal candidate walks through the door, we should be able to peg them right away. Of course, this involves so much more than gender or race.

The avatar begins to take shape with a couple of quick questions you likely already know the answer to:

1. Who on your team would you want to clone? If you don't have a team yet, then think about people whom you have worked with.

2. Who on your team would you happily replace?

Take a look at these people and list some of the characteristics you appreciate, or that drive you nuts. What professional traits do they have? What types of personalities do they have?

You want to ensure diversity in your hiring, having people not only from diverse cultures but also different genders, different ages, and, as I wanted to illustrate here, different personalities. This is the chief reason you don't hire someone just because you get along with them. If your company becomes a back-slapping boys' club of similar thinkers, the party won't last long.

When you ask yourself who to hire, spend some time thinking about the mix of people on your team and describe the "who" that fills the missing part of the puzzle. This will ensure you miss a few landmines in the hiring process.

team input

What does your TEAM think?
Take a minute and run your findings by your leadership or advisory team.
- Do they see the same gaps?
- Do they want to clone the same people?
- Would they fire the same ones as you?
- Why?

Having another point of view while hiring key roles is very useful. Again, it eliminates blind spots. Rookies miss this step and pay for it later on. Take a little time now and reduce poor hiring decisions later.

WHAT ?

Tell me a story
You are sitting at your desk trying to get the last couple lines in on an email when you are told your 10:30 interview is here. As you straighten a few papers, get out a note pad and pull up the resume on your screen, the door opens. Like a scene from a cheesy movie, a beam of light hits them and the Hallelujah Chorus start on cue as the cardboard cutout candidate from step 3 walks through your door and introduces herself.

Stay calm

What story are you going to tell her to win her over?

When something like this happens, most interviewers proceed to talk, no, sell for the next forty minutes, trying to convince the candidate how great their company is. They win them, only to find out later they didn't ask enough questions to discover they were not the right person for the role after all.

Remember: You have two ears and one mouth. Use them in ratio. Talk half as much as you listen. That means, for every half hour interview, you talk only ten minutes and have the candidate talking the other twenty. When someone is allowed to talk about themselves, we learn so much about them, they feel listened to and, therefore, they find you likeable.

What you say to these candidates should be derived from what they want to hear, not just from what you want to tell them. I don't want you to lie to them; you want to focus the story around elements that will resonate with them. A vibrating tuning fork won't break every glass, but it will break the one on the same frequency.

Here's a story: Kevin is your brilliant developer. One of the things he loves best about working with your company is the focus on learning. You have paid for some of his education and encourage him to spend an hour a day reading in his area of interest and one day a month you allow him to work on anything he desires as pure innovation time.

Telling another developer this story in an interview – specifically using one of your current team members as an example – will do more for winning this candidate than almost any salary you may present. If, she is the right one.

ad creation

Extra! Extra! Read all about it!
Now that you have the story, you need to get it out there.

Whatever you do, don't do ads the way most people do.

I know it seems like a good idea to put a ton of information into an ad to try to keep those with no experience from applying. However, that won't work. Get a little cheeky. When you boil down the role to a few key components, saying something like "Don't even think of applying unless you have professional experience dismantling nuclear arms," (if that is what you are looking for). It becomes exclusive in its own way – and shows a little more personality.

Many would argue against putting salary ranges in the ad. You should. It will help the candidate determine if the role is the right level for them.

A key thing to include in your ad is WHY someone would work for you. If you describe the role and company (the good, bad, and ugly), you will find the suitability of candidates applying improve dramatically.

"You can't say the wrong thing to the right person, and you can't say the right thing to the wrong person."

WHERE?

Where have all the good people gone?
Ask the question, "Where can I find the people I am looking for?"

79

Asking peers for referrals is a great starting point. As well, good ads do work.

Let's look at a prioritized list of avenues to win introductions to candidates:

- Implementation of what has been discussed in this book. Healthy companies are attractive.
- Referrals from current employees
- Referrals from GREAT recruiters (because they've taken time to understand your business)
- Referrals from peers
- Referrals from most recruiters
- Responses to your website
- Advertising

There are two approaches to go about finding candidates: Passive and Active

1. Passive recruiting is posting on social networks, indeed, Kijiji/Craigslist/etc., online job boards and your own website.

However, we must get active ourselves to break the barrier to the best people – those who are NOT actively looking. I call them "heads down happy." You must have a different approach to reach the best candidates – the ones who are already working somewhere else.

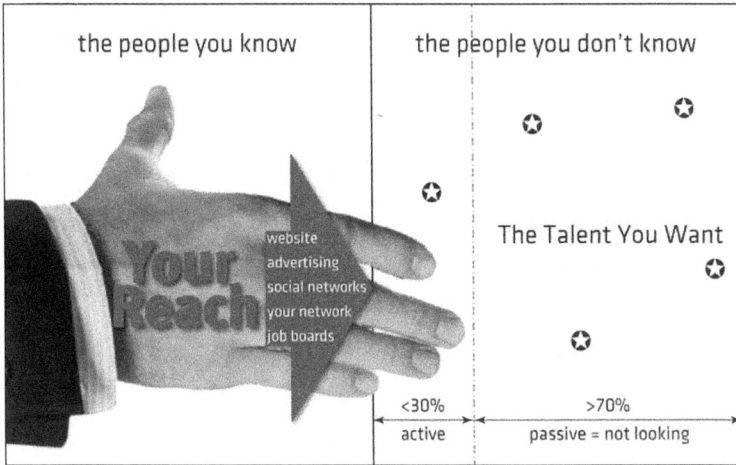

the people you know	the people you don't know
	The Talent You Want
website advertising social networks your network job boards	
<30% active	>70% passive = not looking

2. Active recruiting entails encouraging your team and peers to introduce candidates to the work you do.

Where might they be found? For software developers, User Groups are a good place to start. LinkedIn has thousands of groups, both large and micro, to which your ideal candidate might belong.

Consider looking at your corporate values. If one of your corporate values is social service, getting involved in a Habitat for Humanity build might open some doors for a conversation with new candidates.

Being a part of networking circles at industry events will always help.

Just opening your mouth and sharing about your team, its values and culture, and expressing that you are looking for great people will yield new candidates. Multiply that by the number of people on your team, and you will likely be infinitely more successful than your competition.

Before we get all high and mighty about how that can hurt

other businesses, I want to share a vision I have: Everyone can love what they do. That girl who isn't happy where she is: It does not necessarily mean she is a terrible worker. It might just mean that she has not found what she is looking for. Maybe your role is to help her flourish and love life. That guy you have that doesn't quite fit in: He may be better off released to be with another company. This is all very healthy. It is a shift in mindset - to one of abundance not exclusivity.

recruiting & interviews

Putting it all together

Now that you and your team are out there and candidates are coming in, interviews are being set up. You are seeing the early fruits of your labour.

The interview process is not meant to discover if a candidate is capable of doing the job. Don't hire someone who can do the job; hire someone who is an amazing fit with the team and would LOVE to do the job.

I know this might sound ludicrous when you are having a hard time finding even one good candidate. However, when you get this going properly, the whole process tends to create more candidates.

Therefore, the interview process should distill the pool down to "the one."

First, though, a word about resumes.

Keep in mind that sometimes a resume was written by someone who is very good at writing resumes and not necessarily great at the role needed. I once hired a man who spelled his own name wrong on the resume – true story.

Look for increasing responsibilities across roles. Is your candidate improving or just falling role to role? Look for people who know what it means to make an impact. They often have metrics and details about the difference they made.

The drive-by

I suggest the whole interview process should start with a thirty minute "get to know you" meeting. This can be in your office but is even more effective when done at a neutral place or even somewhere favouring the candidate. You want them to be supremely comfortable because you want them talking like crazy, mostly about themselves. This is not the time to figure out if they can do the job (Competency), but to figure out what type of a person they are. And, most importantly, do they fit in with the team? (Character and Chemistry) Have a few choice questions that will lead into areas you want to go. They must be subtle though; it shouldn't feel too much like an interview.

Of course, you want a few barrier questions that identify if the candidate is even close to what you need. They could be capacity questions and one or two around Competency.

Work at layering questions. Ask a question like, "Have you always lived here?" After they answer, "No, I'm from the Toronto," you can ask, "What brought you here?" This is Hiring 101. For the master class, keep digging to deeper levels such as, "What was the biggest difference you noticed settling in here?" and "Did you change sports team loyalties?"

Another caution - ensure you don't make this all about them. You are building a relationship. If this guy isn't the one, but close, he may have friends and would be willing to help someone he has a relationship with. Do take a few opportunities to talk about yourself, your team, and the role. Finding similarities will do wonders in building trust but work to turn the conversation back to them quickly. Remember the "listen twice as much" part.

The main interview

Once you are happy with the drive-by interview, the candidate moves into more formal interviews.

These should be sixty to ninety minutes and should start with one-on-one. You will not get the best from any candidate in a group or panel interview. Ever. It can make even the most confident person perform poorly. Those who do well are usually good actors or have done so many they are comfortable now.

The power of these interviews will again be in the questions you ask. Although it is important for you to get some answers to technical questions, the first formal interview might not be the best place for that.

These questions should be focused on Character, Chemistry and Capacity. Competency will be determined later in a technical interview.

Asking the right questions will get amazing answers and will reveal so much about the person you want to hire (or avoid). I tailor questions for each of my clients, although these are a starting point for anyone when trying to understand values or character:

- Tell me about a time you had a major failure and how you recovered. This is a great question for those in your leadership team.

- Tell me about where you've put your values to work
- Tell me about a situation where your values were questioned. How did you respond?
- Tell me about a time where your values being reciprocated helped you do better in your role.

Here are a few general questions that will illuminate your candidate:
- Where are you looking to go? (getting a picture for their direction)
- Tell me about your ideal role. (look for the elements that they're describing)
- What elements would you like less of/more of in your new role?
- What makes a great/horrible boss for you?

In all of these, you want to ask deepening questions as well.
- Tell me more about that.
- How did you handle that?
- What happened next?
- What did you learn from that?
- What will you do differently?

Follow the QR Code at the beginning of this hiring section for interview forms, reference checks, onboarding checklists, and monthly check-ins.

Further interviews

Just as you took the role to other members of the team for input, it is a good idea to have others interview your candidates. They might see things you missed or ask a question that reveals something deeper.

You may require deeper technical assessment for specific tools that need expertise. Further interviews to understand these skills can happen here.

Throughout the process, each interviewer must reiterate the values, personality and stories that will resonate with the candidate. They should do this with their own attachment or personal stories that illustrate the values from their experience. They should also be taking copious notes and you should meet to discuss findings and any gaps to ensure you cover what you need in a follow-up interview.

Remember, you cannot make people fall in line with your culture. You have to hire people who are already aligned to your culture. The interview process is there to reveal how well they align to your corporate culture, values and direction. If they are not a GREAT fit, don't move forward with them.

Another element I use for hiring is the same Entrepreneur Assessment from Step 01. It gives a good understanding of the person we are looking to work with. It can also be used with the different team members.

WHEN ?

Now is the time

How do you know it is time to bring them on?

I am sure that when there is a great candidate

going through the process, you cannot seem to reach the offer phase fast enough. Please, slow down and be sure. I know of people who have taken years to be hired. Both the candidate's and company's lives had to get sorted out in due course. It was worth the wait. On the other hand, hiring too quickly has an expensive penalty, both financially and on the culture, which is practically priceless. An important proverb states: "Above all else, guard your heart, for it determines the course of your life." Your corporate culture sets the direction of life for your company. Guard it above all else.

Some considerations for timing:

1. Do you have the finances to pay this candidate? This seems obvious, but the last thing you want to do is rupture your finances for an employee. At the least it could cost your reputation. At the most it could cost you your company.

2. Revisit the WHY from the beginning of this process. Does this hire meet those original outcomes? Or have excitement and other great candidates moved you away from the original goal line?

3. Are there any looming deadlines or projects that will take away from a "wow" onboarding experience for the candidate? No better way to make a bad first impression than the new recruit feeling ostracized or not getting answers to questions or unable to start working in this exciting new company they've joined. Think of a new marriage having to postpone the honeymoon – yikes.

4. Have you truly checked references or only gone through the motions? I sometimes consider references an intelligence test. If someone is stupid enough to give me

a bad reference, they probably shouldn't be working for me. At the same time, if I haven't done them well, who's to blame?

Speaking of references, these days companies can put all sorts of restraints on giving references beyond "he worked for us between so and so dates". Go ahead and ask your questions. Listen for the intangibles, for the tone of voice and also for what isn't being said. I listen for enthusiasm as well.

One more thing about timing. Might there be a way for the candidate to try a project or get involved with your company at a lower or temporary cost to "try before you buy"? This can be good audition for both parties.

Something I encourage every company to do is to have a farm team, a bull pen. You should always be interviewing and meeting qualified candidates. You should go through the process far enough that they are ready to start but when you are ready. When something exciting or urgent happens in your business, you don't want to start a 3 month hiring cycle, you should be ready to make the call to one or more candidates and say "remember me? We're ready for you if you are ready for us."

Your new culture

new culture
negotiation & onboarding

Here we are. We're ready to put ink to paper, to take the plunge, to commit. This is sort of like a marriage.

Unfortunately, commitment and loyalty don't seem as important as they used to and should be.

The idea of someone working at a company for more than a couple of years seems like a distant memory, something we heard about from our parents, or their parents. We've all heard bosses say the Millennials no longer have loyalty and seem to make all these outlandish and seemingly selfish demands. I honestly believe the generation of workers today are NOT the problem. The loyalty issues are not on their side, not completely anyway. They are merely illuminating the problem. There is no loyalty because the organizations are trying to hire cogs instead of intelligent difference makers – linchpins. The shift being seen in the marketplace is because people are looking for something more than just a job and won't stand for being treated like a cog, and it is only a couple years before they are fed up with being unfulfilled and move on.

Remember, bosses may say they want workers who will do what they say, come and go when we want and work as hard as they should. Yet, the "yessir" employees are not the ones who are promoted, receive the raises, and who are given more responsibility. The ones who think for themselves, create opportunities, and are ambitious while still being aligned are the ones rewarded. Don't buy into the lie. Who would you really rather hire?

We will have loyalty when we work alongside the team members rather than above them, when we collaborate with their wisdom and experience and see the intelligence of the whole as greater than the sum of its parts, when we look after our team members as if they are our immediate family – with respect and love and care and concern for their wellbeing.

This brings us to negotiation and winning the candidates of your dreams. If all the rest of the Steps have been done successfully, this step is relatively easy.

Negotiation with the right person is easy. With the wrong person, it is all about money. If your discussion is not going well, ask yourself what you might have missed. It is never too late to say, "Sorry, you're not the right fit for us." Zappos, as part of their final interview process, offers the candidates $2000 cash to walk away right then and there, and not accept the position. This weeds out those who are interested in the money rather than the long-term experience. Two thousand dollars is much less expensive than the cost of a poor hire.

A good hire will improve your culture. A bad hire will undo everything you have built.

Remuneration

Understand enough of your market to ensure you know what is fair. Offer what is fair and there is no need to go above that. The goal for pay should be what is fair and what will allow the candidate to pay their bills comfortably. If they are constantly stressed about money, good luck getting them to focus on work.

Remember, the right candidate is motivated intrinsically by the work they are doing at your company, and by the team they get to be a part of.

Now that you have gone this far down the path together, salary discussions do not need to be rival poker players shielding their hand from the other. It is not taboo to have an open talk about the needs on both sides and come to a mature agreement. How candidates handle this may indicate more about them and reveal their real motivation as well.

Bonuses should be that: an unexpected random bonus, financial or otherwise, recognising behaviour you want repeated. This would include exceptional sales, examples of corporate values, and great teamwork. Think of imaginative ways to give bonuses.

An alternative is **profit sharing** as it really demonstrates your conviction to have them own the business - there must be profit in order to have profit "sharing." This may help motivate employees to work in partnership with you.

Increases can be given annually or when consistent changes in responsibility or performance dictate it.

Think about how you justify these items more than just a blanket approach dismissed as "the way we are supposed to do it." A little key mentioned earlier is how do you reward the behaviour you want repeated?

Back when I was recruiting, as a team we would get a bonus if we hit our numbers. Each month we hit our numbers, and rather than spend it each month, we decided to keep saving it to build towards something big. It was summer by the time we decided to spend it. We ended up renting a few very sporty cars for the day. Once we got the cars, we met for a nice breakfast and spent the day racing around, taking turns driving in between events. The guys went to a men's spa and the women went to their own spa, both for our choice of relaxation. More driving, more food, and later we went to a great dinner together, and ended up at a casino with a few hundred dollars each to play with. One of the most memorable workdays ever.

Onboarding

It is not a surprise when someone is coming onboard. Hopefully, everyone will know a new team member will be starting well in advance of their first day, so the rest of your team should be ready to welcome them.

A checklist

- ☐ Are their computer and desk ready?
- ☐ Who needs to get time with them to show them the ropes?
  - ☐ Administration
  - ☐ Paydays
  - ☐ Protocols
  - ☐ Technology
  - ☐ Benefits
  - ☐ Training
- ☐ Who will be their mentor and go-to person for the first few weeks?
- ☐ What dates are in the calendar for one-week check-in, one-month check-in, three-month, six-month, nine-month and one-year check-ins? Who will they be having these meetings with?
  - ☐ What are they noticing in the team, company and culture?
  - ☐ How are things measuring up to their expectations?
  - ☐ What's working and what isn't?
  - ☐ What would they like to improve?
  - ☐ What might I, the boss, improve? (Yes, you should be asking this.)
  - ☐ Where are the corporate values being shown? Where they are not?

☐   When are you – as the owner – going to meet with them and share your story and vision for the company one-on-one?

These are all important. You have spent time and energy getting the right person, it would be a shame to not back up all you have promised and lose them, and the $50,000 it takes to replace them, not including any potential damage to the team and clients that may be affected.

Every new person you bring to the team affects the culture.

Organize your Team

Once you have a team, everyone needs to be aligned around the Vision, Mission, Values and Goals of the business. Here is how to organize them and get them all rowing in the same direction.

How do we know who does what?

Accountabilities chart

Typically, companies have an organizational chart. These are good, but they do not go far enough.

When you are first building a team, I suggest you map out all the things that need to get done-day in and day-out in your organization and start categorizing them. The financial needs and administrative will end up being together, the sales and marketing responsibilities will often group together, as will all the operational and production responsibilities.

When you already have a team in place, it is tricky to separate what you already have – what people are doing certain things – from what the ideal situation could be. This is best done with a few hours to yourself imagining what you would do if you were to start all over. How would you re-structure your team? Remember to start without names. Just focus on grouping the responsibilities that need to get done day-in and day-out.

As these responsibilities come together, you can go as detailed as you want. However, once you get everything mapped out and organized, each role should come down to between three and seven responsibilities. If you have more than that, you either have too many responsibilities for one person or you are micro-defining the role that might also lead to micromanaging the person in the role. If you have too few, you either have too many positions listed for that role or have not defined the role deeply enough.

The human brain can easily remember up to seven items, like the digits in a telephone number. After that, things get missed. Having a list of seven things each team member is responsible for each day will allow them to understand if they are being successful.

Once you have created a responsibility chart, you can start adding names. You may find that the roles are miscast, or certain people have too much on their plate. If you are just starting your business, your name is probably in every box for now.

If you are creating a new chart from an old one, you and the leadership team will need to plan how to get everything shifted around to get the roles corrected. This will take some time, but it is worth it.

Now you have your people organized on paper. How do you keep it moving?

CORE 4 meetings

Every business has a rhythm.

Like breathing, like life itself, your business should have a healthy rhythm. Not too fast, not too slow. The rhythm is put in place by the leadership and is maintained by everyone.

Getting this rhythm right, like running a marathon, is vital to the health of the company. Too fast and people burn out. Too slow and things are not getting done at the pace the customer needs.

The rhythm – like a back beat – is set in motion by the CORE 4 meetings.

Good meetings are time savers. Bad meetings suck time and life out of the people. Proper meetings accelerate decision making which saves everyone from dealing with the same issues over and over and never really solving them – which is what most meetings seem like. When done properly, they are fun, effective and create a tempo the whole business can dance/work to.

The CORE 4 meetings are:

- The daily check-in
- The weekly tactical
- The quarterly offsite
- The ad hoc strategic

The Daily Check-in

I suggest you book these in for at least two months to get it into a habit. If they are done properly, they will grow in attendance and you will see improvements in communication throughout your teams.

These can be held with up to about ten people in each group. Walmart does this with everyone, and it is a little much – yet it still works for them. Ten people should allow for fifteen minutes maximum.

Have these meetings standing up and at the same time and place each day.

The question of what happens if people are out of the office for meetings with clients comes up a fair bit. I would suggest that everyone meets first and then goes to meetings. This meeting can work by phone as well. If someone is not there, just have the meeting anyway with whomever is. Do not lose the tempo just because someone is not there. One person and the leader make for a fine meeting and doing this well will make it infectious.

There are a few things that happen as a benefit to this style of meeting: Communication goes up because there is an opportunity every day to discuss burning issues. It also creates a more cohesive office when everyone is seeing each other briefly each day. It is like eating together as a family every night. Finally, the greatest benefit is that everyone knows what everyone else is working on and can weigh in and help out when needed.

The format of the meeting is simple. There are two questions posed to each person from the leader:

1. What do you need to get done today?
2. How can I help you?

This might seem like it is going to fill up your to-do list faster than anything. However, the team will not abuse this when they discover your sincerity. It may take some coaching one on one with your team members if they are pulling you in for items below your pay grade. Ideally, you will see through that right in the meeting and ask them a question or two to help them work it out on their own.

The times when they do require your help, you will be able to clear paths for them or introduce them to someone who can help. It might be someone inside the company or outside.

In small and/or young teams, this meeting is essential. I believe it should never be stopped; however, it is especially important for new and/or small teams.

Culture and getting things done are the most important elements in business. This daily meeting will do more for your culture and activity than almost anything else. It breeds a culture of getting things done, one where each person knows what the other is working on and everyone knows they have some help from the leader when needed.

The leader has to see this as a non-negotiable. Set it up right from the beginning and it will become part of the fabric of the company. Before long, you will wonder how anyone can do without it.

The Weekly Tactical

The weekly tactical meeting should be an all-hands company meeting.

With everyone together, the leadership paints the vision, mission, values, and goals, rewards those exemplifying them, and keeps the business working between the rails.

I have heard the CEO role defined as the CRO role: The Chief Reminder Officer. I like this because it shows the value of constantly reminding the people of where they are going, how they get there, who they serve and what's important right now. Laying these things out for people weekly is undeniably powerful. Try it.

With a weekly tactical meeting of eight to twelve people or even fewer, it becomes – well - very tactical. Everyone can weigh-in and there can be tight accountability. But, if everyone starts listing out every project they're working on and the details needed, it would take far too long.

The other thing about this weekly tactical meeting is it should always be the same. It must start and stop exactly on time. Never go over the 90 minutes and never start late. If someone is late, it will be obvious. If they do not feel the shame of being late, someone will need to talk with them. This meeting can become a very strong tool in being effective as a team.

I like to point out at the beginning of these meetings that it is a "hats off zone." Silos are killers in business and when Sal is fighting for his team to get funding or attention, it is painful for everyone. These meetings require everyone to take off their departmental hats and focus on what is best for the company.

Here is the 90-minute weekly agenda I use:

- Five minutes to shift from work to the meeting – ice breaker, selected small talk
- Five minutes to review the key metrics for the company – pure stats, no commentary
- Five minutes to announce any headlines – what is new, important, interesting, good news etc.
- Five minutes to review quarterly projects. Each person in the room should have projects they are working on, and simply gives a "red light," "yellow light," "green light" status. Red means it is stopped. Yellow means it has an issue, Green means all is good. This whole process is rapid fire.
- Five minutes to do the same Red, Yellow, Green scoring on weekly must-dos for each person. These are the big things that must get done inside or outside projects that are important to the company. Obviously, they were created at last week's meeting.
- Sixty minutes to thrash solutions. This is the opportunity for projects, problems, threats and whatnot to get solved, moving and squashed.
- Five minutes to review the next steps and discuss communication. How will it be communicated, to whom using what format by whom? Then, close with rating the meeting out of 10, then close. Level 10 meetings end with the rating. If you are consistently below an 8, you might want to reconsider the structure to the meeting. No more boring meetings… ever.

The Quarterly Off-site

These are very powerful and company-moving meetings. There are two versions.

1. Annual full-day or two-day planning session. You guessed it, once a year
2. Regular, half-day or full-day, quarterly planning sessions. Three times a year

Annual Full-day Planning session

How to have a successful Annual Planning Session.

Two weeks in advance

- Confirm attendance, venue, and timing.
- Have each member work through the elements of Step 01. This does not have to be shared. It will help your leadership team mature personally and create good discussions in one-on-ones and result in more engaged team members.
- Have each member of the group fill in the One-Page Business Blueprint.
- Get assessments done. This includes DiSC, Social Styles, Colours, Insights, MBTI, and a few others. You might use the assessments from Step 01 or Step 05.

The Event

Ice Breaker

I like to open the day with some questions that get the team more unified.

1. Where were you born? (city, country)
2. How many siblings and where are you in the mix?
3. What was the most interesting or difficult challenge and lesson learned as a child? (looking for childhood memories, not inner child)

You can Google speed-dating questions for more ideas rather than the same questions each year.

Discuss the findings of the Personality Assessment. For thirty minutes go around the room and have each person share their personality assessment and how accurate they see it. They may share what the most surprising aspect was.

Work through the elements of the Six Questions

1. What is the problem we are solving? Step 02
   a. Why do we exist?
   b. Who are we solving it for – our hero?
   c. How can we define it better?
   d. How are we making the world better?
   e. What difference are we making?
   f. What would go away if we went away?
   g. Create our journey for the hero we guide
2. What are the company values?
   a. What are we willing to be punished for?
   b. What won't we stand for?
   c. Where do we see these values exemplified?
   d. Where do we see them being stomped on?

e. How can we get the company to reflect the values we hold?

3. How do we measure our success?

a. Define the marketing strategy

b. Define the sales process

c. What measures are important to us?

d. How do we tell if we are winning?

e. What are early indicators to success and failure?

4. Where are we going?

a. How do we create a vision the team is excited about?

b. What is a short memorable story about what we do as a company?

5. How will we get there?

a. What are the three-year foundational pillars?

b. What do we want to accomplish in the next 365 days?

c. What is most important for the next 90 days?

i. Get everyone to share their view from the 1PBB and discuss pros and cons of each one. Get unified on the best one.

ii. A way to state this: What is the one thing such that, if we could accomplish it, would make all the other things moot?

d. Define the 90-day projects needed to get there

6. Who does what?

a. Review or design an accountability chart

b. Discuss key roles and current team members using the People Fit Tool.

c. Create a strategy around building the right team

Cascading communication
1. How are the outcomes going to be communicated?
2. What are the main messages?
3. Who communicates what to who?
4. What is the communication tree to ensure the whole organization hears everything clearly and consistently and timely?

Once the first Annual Planning session is done, the future annual ones become a review and refocus through these elements. Some will be refined and improved. Values may be more clearly stated.

More time will be spent on the improving the metrics you use to monitor the company, how to improve the numbers, discussions around key roles, who to hire, who to relieve and how to create a better culture and more successful team. You will also spend more time on building out the big projects to get to those three-year foundational pillars, the one-year elements and new projects.

Regular Half-day Planning session

The regular quarterly meetings begin with a review of the Vision, Mission, Values and Goals.

Next comes the review of the three-year foundational pillars from Step 04, the quarterly breakdown, and a good discussion of "what is most important now."

New projects get created and detailed, then assigned and communication processes set to get out to the team at large.

The Ad Hoc Strategic

This meeting is quite straightforward. It deals with anything that comes up in a daily or weekly or quarterly meeting - or even something in a one-on-one meeting that needs a deeper dive - becomes an Ad Hoc Strategy meeting.

The focus of this meeting is one agenda item. Anyone there is there only to help solve this issue. It may happen in five minutes; it may take five hours and you will need to order lunch. Only the people who need to be in the room should be there. This is neither a department meeting nor a team meeting. It is called strictly to solve a single strategic issue.

STEP 06 – Process and Duplication

This section is most important in maturing businesses, businesses that are getting ready to be handed off, or ones where the owner is looking to pull back from the business. However, new businesses should keep these ideas in mind as it is easier to "bake" it in from the beginning.

Passing the Bus Test

I refer to this step as "Passing the Bus Test." If you – or anyone in your organization – gets hit by a bus, can someone step in and take over the role seamlessly? That could be someone else on the team or someone coming in from the outside. No one is ever ready to be hit by a bus but the more mature a company is, the more resilient it is to unforeseen impacts.

The best franchises are an example of the duplicatable processes I am talking about. A franchise is just a well-documented and thought-through plan on how to ensure every role knows what to do, then carries it out.

The "[your-company-name-here] way" is another term for it. How do we do things here? This document or corporate manual is updated regularly and followed by all.

You should be able to hand it to someone who would be able to open the business and follow the manual to success. It is like an instruction manual for someone who has never used it before. Some of us can be good at opening something new and not having to read the manual. For some, this is a necessity. For business, it should be a necessity. There are too many moving parts to be simply plug-and-play.

The biggest benefit of getting this Step right is increasing the value of the business.

Contrast this to a business where all the secrets to success are in the owner's head. This fails the bus test. The owner gets hit by a bus, and the business goes away with the owner because no one else knows how to run it as well as they did.

The way you do things should be captured and followed – by everyone – even you. It will improve and refine until it is clearly a differentiating advantage. At every stage, you want your team to follow the processes and to improve them constantly. First you need to start documenting them.

The best book I have read on this is Built to Sell by John Warrillow where our protagonist takes a graphic design business from something only he can run to a very valuable company for the next owner. The difference is several zeros from the beginning to end.

Here is how to document the processes of your business.

Identify

The first thing you need to do is to Identify the core processes you will be working with. It might be the recipe for your muffins or how a product is made in a machine shop. What areas are you going to document first? What areas will you tackle and when? Consider HR, Marketing, Sales, the different Operational areas, Accounting, Customer Service, Technology etc.

Consider how each department works and what their core operations need to be. The accountability chart from earlier is a start to this. Each person has a set of responsibilities and those fit into the bigger whole. Each person has a number/ metric they are responsible for and that also fits into the bigger picture.

Give each document a name and have everyone agree to use that name.

Document

Once you identify the areas and a timeline for each one, now you record the major steps in each of the above processes. Focus on them in a linear/chronological approach. What happens first? What happens next? What do you need to have to do this? What tools and materials are required? What do the outcomes look like? What measures will tell you if you are on the right track or have done it properly?

Have a few people who know the process try it and share feedback. Have a few people who know little about the process try it and share feedback. Someone new should be able to work off the document and accomplish the outcomes required.

Package

Combine each documented CORE process into a binder or online tool for easy accessibility and reference. Everyone who works with that process needs to easily access it and follow it. And, be graded on it.

The list of CORE processes from the IDENTIFY step should be the Table of Contents.

Give the package a name: "The [My-Business] Way"

Project Planning

Part of maturing your business is executing proper projects rather than just winging what needs to get done each month.

Here is an outline for how to have successful projects such as we discussed in Step 04.

Project Tracking

Tracking and holding accountability around those projects should be done at each weekly meeting. An example of a project tracking log is available online.

Q6 Debrief

One last aspect to maturing your company through process: The Q6 Debrief.

I have seen companies that implement just this tool after every project, every event, every milestone, make unbelievable progress.

The six questions are:

Where did we win?

Why did we win?

Where did we lose?

Why did we lose?

Where do we need to go from here?

How do we get there?

The tool online has more indepth questions as well.

STEP 07 - Delegate and Improve

The whole idea of this book and the visual design of The Entrepreneur Roadmap is a lemniscate… an infinity loop. After we have gone through these seven steps once, we go back and do it all again, getting deeper, growing in our understanding. We never stop planning and working on us. We never stop learning and refining about our relationships with our clients, we can always improve our financial understanding, metrics and measures. We are building a PhD in our business. Our plan for Step 04 is always extending and refining. We are constantly improving our teams, the culture and story. The Company Way is never done.

That brings us to delegation and improvement. The Japanese have a term for this: Kaizen – constant improvement, the idea that we are always able to tweak and improve.

The core aspects of this step are delegation, solving big problems, measuring our current state and starting from the beginning again.

Kaizen /ˈkī zə n/ Noun: a Japanese business practice of continuous improvement in performance and productivity. Best implemented with the process: **PDSA: Plan * Do * Study * Act**

The simple version of Kaizen is the Q6 Debrief. One way I like to work through things is to start with a blank canvas. What I mean is, if you had to start your business over today, knowing all that you have learned so far, what would you do differently?

Delegate

Our business is limited to the degree we delegate.

If everything rides on our shoulders, not only does it fail the bus test, but it also means we are tied to our business for as long as it continues.

The secret to success is to delegate anything we as the leader do not need to do.

When it comes to delegation, the first thing to consider is this: What is it that only you and no one else can do?

No one can be father to my kids. It is all mine and I cannot delegate that. I don't want anyone else to be husband to my wife. Until I leave this earth, my responsibility is to be a husband and father. I can hire someone to do the lawn or fix the roof: I cannot, and should not, delegate the roles of husband and father.

In business, there are also things that only we can do. Our job as owners is to identify what those few things are and to determine how to make them as few as possible.

Likely, no one can create the vision like you do. No one can inspire the team like you can. No one can tell the story of the business like you can. These are all elements that may fit your specific role. Delegate everything else as much as possible for greater success and freedom.

Take some time to work through the delegation tool found online in Step 07.

Take the form and enter all the responsibilities you have. You can use the responsibilities you already know, and there are a number of extra ones on the list above as well as another page

in the worksheet available online. Each responsibility should go into one of the quadrants.

The quadrants are divided into those that give you energy and those that suck your energy. Then, each of those are divided into those you are good at and those you are not good at. A simplified version might look like this.

Love and Great at	Like and Not Good at
Like and Good at	Don't like and Not Good at

You want to avoid the bottom right hand corner. Make sure you delegate those. Ideally, you want to focus only on the top left quadrant.

It must be said that just handing things off does not fix the delegation problem. You must delegate to good people (covered in Step 05) and continually train and coach them to be the best they can be.

There does need to be a certain level of trust, and room for error. I often say entrepreneurs need to be comfortable with a certain level of chaos. Just remember when you were starting in business and how many mistakes you made – and it still worked! Do not be afraid to trust your people's intuition and let them fail occasionally. If you have good meeting rhythm and good communication, you can usually catch things before they get too far off track.

Trust is essential to delegation.

Solve Big Problems

When you're ready to solve big problems, use this process to thrash them and solve them. You should come out of this with a solution to any problem you clearly identify.

This process works best as a framework in the Ad Hoc meeting from Step 05.

Identify

The problem brought up is rarely the real issue. You have to dig to discover the real issue. So you must keep digging until you clearly identify the issue. Don't move on until you clearly identify the real issue.

This is a lot like Step 02. The better you can define the problem, the easier the solution is. Once the real issue is identified, only then do you move to the discussion section.

Discuss

While discussing, do not allow tangents. This will take major discipline and practice. Give everyone latitude to simply say "tangent" and bring everyone back on track. The environment needs to be open and honest. Everyone must be free to share their thoughts, ideas, concerns, and solutions without personal attacks. Understand the difference between a critical eye and a critical heart. It is good to thrash the ideas and get to the best solutions.

Discuss and debate until everything is out on the table.

Work to get everything out on the table. The point being made should only be said once, though. Otherwise, it is politicking. Once the parts to the problem become redundant. It is time to move to the solution. Always keep the greater good in mind. It is not personal, it is for the betterment of the business.

Now that the parts of the problem are clear, it is time to solve it.

Solve

It is more important to decide rather than what you decide. You must leave with a decision. Leadership is not always about the right direction; it's about choosing the best direction at the time.

Keep stating different solutions until there is agreement and heads nodding. Sometimes you will need to return to DISCUSS because you might not be solving the real problem.

Agreement doesn't mean everyone is 100% with the solution. It means everyone can live with the decision and will support it 100%.

There needs to be clear Must Do's and someone needs to own the solutioning project. It is not a solution until someone owns the Must Do's and there is a clear communications plan to those who are affected by it.

There also needs to be a clear communication strategy. Who will say what? When will it be said by? How will it be delivered? "Kevin will announce it at the next team meeting on Tuesday. He will deliver it live, with supporting slide deck. We will also put it in the newsletter."

Everyone should be able to state in a clear paragraph what is to be said. If you go around the room and everyone says what they heard, you are likely to find a few miscommunications. Go back to it until everyone can agree on what is being delivered.

Note: 80% of the time everyone agrees. 20% they don't and the CEO needs to make the final decision. Make sure everyone is heard and most will be fine with and – ultimately – support the decision.

Decision Making

In the book Entreleadership the author Dave Ramsay gives an excellent checklist for making decisions. Seth Godin also uses a few great ideas to make decisions.

Use this framework as a foundation to help you solve any problems and make better decisions.

Good decisions are made in spite of fear. Maybe what you have to decide on is not fun. Acknowledge that and that you would rather not be in this situation… and move on.

It is okay to be passively active. Waiting to decide is still a decision. Strategic procrastination. Remember Step 01 for getting things done.

Take time equal to the size of the decision: a big decision takes longer; a short decision should not take long at all.

Set a self-imposed calendar deadline if one doesn't naturally occur.

Get options… and more options. The with the most information makes the best decisions. None are likely perfect.

Comparing the options gives us objective decisions.

Clearly state (or review) your values. This helps make decisions that align with them.

Break the decision into smaller bites. Some decisions can be intimidating. Start with smaller parts and they are easier to decide.

Determine the financial implications of the decision. Ignore sunk costs. They are exactly that – sunk. They should have no impact on the decision you need to make

Always ask real experts – that have the heart of the teacher. You will learn more from someone who has a heart of a teacher, and thus, making better decisions in the future as you learn how others wrestle with it.

Seek the counsel of your spouse – this is very wise. My wife has such a different perspective than me, it is often refreshing – sometimes a little frustrating, too.

If all else fails, write yourself an objective report as you would to a boss or someone else you want to help make the decision. This works to get it out of your head.

Questions for better decisions

The first question here is from an incredible lesson called "Ask It" by Andy Stanley.

"In light of your PAST experiences,
your CURRENT situation,
and your FUTURE hopes and dreams
– what is the WISE thing to do?"

1. Define the problem
2. Why does the problem exist?
3. How does the problem present itself?
4. How is the problem currently being solved?
5. Why is it important to solve it?
6. What is working? Why?
7. What isn't working? Why?
8. Quantify the problem. How much does it cost? How much does it hurt? How wide is it?
9. How would the solution make your life better?
10. What are your values around this problem?
11. When does the decision NEED to be made?
12. Who are the experts you can talk to about this?
13. What has your spouse said about it?
14. What is the desired outcome?

Q20

If you have not taken this with your now up-and-running business, it is time to take this quiz. Or, take it again and see how it has changed through the process of working through this book. Do this regularly to get some encouragement on what is changing and what still needs to be done.

To the ever-increasing value of your business.

PART III – OVERVIEW

This section summarizes the important learning elements of each step and the quick tips and homework for each tool.

Step 01

Know what you want your life to look like before you choose a business.

Blueprint Your Life

Quick Tip
Most people spend more time planning a one-week vacation than they do their life. Know what you stand for, what needs focus and what is most important to you.

Action to take
Book three hours, your favourite drink, no distractions and work through the tool.

7Fs

Quick Tip
Take two minutes and grade how you feel about each of these areas

Action to take
To make significant change, take the results from here into "Blueprint your life" and set plans on how to improve each one.

Get Stuff Done

Quick Tip

Eliminate distractions and exercise a few simple tricks and you can be more productive

Action to take

Try the End of Day Planning, Must Do's and 55|5 for three days

Ideal Week

Quick Tip

Imagine a week where everything you needed to get done fit in. What would it look like?

Action to take

Take one hour and plan a weekly rhythm that fits the core elements in each week.

Buckets

Quick Tip

Know what fills and empties your buckets

Action to take

Book twenty minutes to go through this exercise.

Entrepreneur Assessment

Quick Tip
Know yourself so you can understand where you are strong and where you need help from others.

Action to take
Take thirty minutes and do an overview on you and where you will need support

Step 02

Build something people want. There is no substitute for talking with prospective customers.

Know your Customers

Quick Tip
What is the real problem you are solving? Not just an idea but bring life to the real problem and how it affects your customer. The biggest competitor is usually status quo. The real problem might not be the first thing you think it is. Prove this is something people want by getting Non-Binding LOIs (Letters of Intent). This will help with confidence and investors.

Action to take
Work through this document. At the very least, go find ten customers with whom the problem resonates with the

problem and ask lots of questions to understand why the problem exists.

Value Curve Analysis

Quick Tip

Be clear on the very specific areas you are different. What are you competing against, really? Don't choose price. Find the niche where you fit.

Action to take

Talk with your customers about their decision-making processes. How do you compare on several different areas? Purchases are not single dimension.

Empathy Map

Quick Tip

Get into the head of your customer. Know what they hear, see and think.

Action to take

Sit down with one engaged customer prospect and work through this with them.

Customer Journey

Quick Tip

You need to know all the channels through which the customer might find you. Once they show interest, what materials, people, choices, do they need to experience to make the buying decision?

Action to take

Put yourself in the shoes of a client, better still, sit down with one and work through the experience of finding and buying something. Break it into steps, parts, people, materials, content, etc.

Step 03

Make sure you can build and deliver it for less than you charge for it. Make sure the business is viable and not just a hobby.

Cash Flow Analysis

Quick Tip

You must have a firm understanding of how the money moves in and out of your business. Not just a budget but what days the transactions happen.

Action to take

Take one hour to input all your recurring incomes and expenses. Add any upcoming extraneous income and expenses and look at the graphs. How will you make up any differences needed?

Go, No Go

Quick Tip

Get very good at making an assumption, proving or disproving it in as little time and money as possible and then pivoting if needed. Know when you should decide if this business has a chance. It is okay to stop if it can't work. Get non-binding LOI's from your customers and investors. When you have several, you have traction.

Action to take

Put some time into figuring out how you can prove one part of your business. Examine the beginnings of Zappos, Dinner Dash, and how GE innovates.

Scorecard

Quick Tip

Your business should have a few numbers that are indicators to the current and future health of your business. Cash flow is one. There are different ones for different types of businesses. Always have them at your fingertips.

Action to take

Think through your business. What are the things that make a difference each day in your success? Write them down. How will you collect them? How will you act on them?

Budget Template

Quick Tip

Capture every possible income and outgo of your business monthly and annually... and even longer.

Action to take

Take an hour and put together a working accurate budget for your next year.

Step 04

Create the big vision and work backwards to today. Make sure everyone has a ninety-day plan.

Telescope to Microscope

Quick Tip

Start planning with the end in mind. What do you want the business to look like in five-ten years and work backwards from there to what needs to be done today

Action to take

Take a couple hours and spend the first part dreaming of what can be. Then, work through the document. Create a few key projects and find an accountability partner to start checking in with. Call that person a mentor.

One-Page Business Blueprint

Quick Tip

Put all you know about your business onto this one pager for your memory and to share with others.

Action to take

Fill in the One-Page Business Blueprint and review it weekly.

Implementation Planner

Quick Tip

Investors (and you) want to know what needs to be done each quarter and how much it will cost.

Action to take

Create a six to eight quarter implementation plan (including budgets needed) using the projects from Telescope to Microscope.

Step 05

Never hire out of convenience. Fit is more important than talent. People rally around VMVG (Vision, Mission, Values, Goals).

Create Alignment

Quick Tip

Understand what each role needs to do and how to measure the success of each role. Clearly explain it and hold each team member accountable to the plan.

Action to take

Use the example in the tool and create an org chart for your business. Imagine it in a few years when operating the way you want. How will you organize what will be done? Each role should only have five to seven responsibilities.

People Fit Tool

Quick Tip

Fit and culture is more important than skills. Measure objectively.

Action to take

Pick one or more on your team (contractors too) and use this tool to get an objective score.

Weekly Agenda

Quick Tip

Your weekly meetings with your team should happen at the same time, at the same place and

cover the same things ... including accountability on projects for each person

Action to take
Put together an agenda using this tool and run one meeting with it.

Core 4 Meetings

Quick Tip
You should only ever have four types of meetings: Strategic quarterly offsites, weekly operational team meetings, daily standing quick updates, Single-agenda item ad hoc meeting as needed.

Action to take
Sit down and schedule out a year of quarterly meetings. Pick the best time, day and location for your weekly team meeting and who should attend. Commit to one week of daily check-ins.

Leadership Matrix

Quick Tip
There are key roles you need in leadership. Someone should be responsible for each of these areas. Not only is their personal success important, the ability of the team working together is also key.

Action to take

Take thirty minutes and work through this tool. How can you make your leadership team better?

Entrepreneur Assessment

Quick Tip

Know your team well. They are the most important part of your success. Understand their personalities, talents, culture, and how to motivate them.

Action to take

Get each team member to fill in the form and spend some time with each one reviewing it and asking questions about them and their answers.

Hiring Blueprint

Quick Tip

Slow down the hiring process and make sure you hire someone that is good for the team culturally, not just for their skills.

Action to take

Read through The Hiring Blueprint for an important overview.

131

HBP – WHY are you hiring?

Quick Tip
Know why you are hiring for this role.

Action to take
Answer the questions in the included form.

HBP – Describe WHAT needs to be done

Quick Tip
Write out a list of everything you want this role to do. What does success look like for this role?

Action to take
Review the accountability chart in Step 05 and create the must do's for success in this role.

HBP – WHO is ideal person?

Quick Tip
Define the qualities of others you would want to clone.

Action to take
Create a list of qualities about the people you have loved to work with in the past.

HBP – Get feedback from the team

Quick Tip
Get more eyes on the role and the need. Review with your team and/or mentor.

Action to take
Review your ideas from the previous steps with a peer or mentor.

HBP – What will you tell the ideal candidate?

Quick Tip
If you were to tell a story to the perfect person, what would you say to them?

Action to take
Create a compelling story about the team and the role and where you are going as a company and why it's exciting to be here.

HBP – Create the ideal ad

Quick Tip
A job ad should be compelling and exciting.

Action to take
Create a job ad and have a few people review it.

HBP – WHERE will you find your ideal person?

Quick Tip

Treat your hiring like your marketing. Understand your employees' and prospects' motivations, interests, where they like to go and where they would like to work.

Action to take

Do an empathy map from Step 02 for your ideal candidate.

HBP – HOW to do the ideal interviews

Quick Tip

Start with a quick phone interview or a neutral spot for coffee. Then do a cultural interview about the person. Then do a technical interview about their skills.

Action to take

Create some quick conversational questions to determine the most important things you want to know, as well as what you would share to excite them. Determine how to have the ideal candidates audition for the role.

HBP – WHEN is the best time to bring them on?

Quick Tip

Check budgets, cash flows and the employee's team mentor and other elements to be sure.

Action to take
Make a pitch to your mentor about how you plan to pay for and keep paying for this employee, as well as how you will keep them engaged.

HBP - Create your ideal culture

Quick Tip
Create an exciting first impression with everything as you would want to be romanced and onboarded.

Action to take
Write out your perfect hiring experience. Who would you meet? What would you want to do the first day? What do you want to know? Ask someone else as well.

Step 06

Make sure your business passes the bus test. If someone gets hit by a bus, can things keep going?

Build Processes

Quick Tip
You should have something to hand each person describing "how we do it here." The more your business is systemized, the easier it is to manage and the more valuable it becomes.

Action to take

Pick one role in your company and write down the ideal way you want it to be done. Consult with the expert doing it if you need to. The instructions are in the tool.

Project Planner

Quick Tip

Structuring a project in the right way will help it to have more successful outcomes.

Action to take

Put together a project using this framework from the Telescope to Microscope tool earlier.

Q6 Debrief

Quick Tip

Take a moment after a project or a meeting and reflect on how it went.

Action to take

This is so simple. There are six questions. Carry this in your back pocket and ask them after each meeting and each project.

Project Tracking Log

Quick Tip

You need to keep track of the projects that are on the go and who is responsible for them and how much they cost.

Action to take

Use this at your weekly meeting to get updates from each person.

Step 07

The role of a leader is to delegate everything but the ONE thing you are good at.

Kaizen

Quick Tip

The secret to making something awesome is constant little improvements. Do something every day to improve your business in some way.

Action to take

What is the biggest thing you want to see improved in your business or life? What can you do today to move it even just 1%? Make it happen.

Delegation

Quick Tip

The leader should only focus on a couple areas where they make the biggest impact. Everything else should be delegated.

Action to take

Take a couple hours and spend the first part dreaming of what can be. Then, work through the document. Create a few key projects and find an accountability partner to start checking in with. This could be your mentor.

Solve Big Problems

Quick Tip

Big problems are intimidating. They can be solved with a little time and effort.

Action to take

Pick a single problem you want solved and get your team (or advisors) in a room and work though this tool once.

Make Better Decisions

Quick Tip

Making good decisions is important for the leader. The one with the most information makes the best decisions.

Action to take
Pick something you have been having trouble making a decision on and work through this tool once.

Q20

Quick Tip
Regularly check in on the current health of the business. It is easy to let it get away from you. Work ON the business, rather than only IN the business.

Action to take
Go fill in this tool for your current business. Identify the parts you scored the lowest and pick a relevant tool, book some time to work through and implement it.

Acknowledgements

I could quite literally write another book just for acknowledgements. There are so many people that have helped me to understand life, relationships, business and myself. Some have had the courage to call me out when I was a doofus or let me fall on my face to learn what I needed to. Others have helped me carry burdens too much for one man. Still others have been the quiet calm when I was losing it. I find that I have learned a lot from almost everyone and I feel terrible that I have left so many people out. Here are a few that really stand out.

My faith in God has been forged in fire and to him be all the glory and honour.

I cannot fathom the wisdom God has in allowing me to find my wife Melissa. She is perfect for me in every way. She has a very well-tuned security gland that has somehow survived through all these years of insecurity. Her insight of people and situations has rescued me from doing foolish things more times than I can count. Her thinking completes mine. I don't feel like I have thought through something completely without her insights.

My kids are amazing. It has been a joy being around to watch them grow up and I only hope the ups and downs financially haven't scarred them permanently.

A few of my many mentors: Lindsay Dodd, Dan Duckering, Edi Balian, Tom Ogaranko, Warren Bergen, Dragan Marjanovic, Shawn Brown, Richard Bourne.

A huge thank you to my editor, Trevor McMonagle, who greatly improved every aspect of this book making it so much better to read and easier to understand. I am wordy at the best of times and he made it coherent.

Thank you also to my clients, my friends, my family and my parents. You are my life support.

Finally, to entrepreneurs everywhere that I have talked with, listened to, seen examples of, and been inspired by. This book is for our kind to thrive.

Author Biography

Colin Christensen is a serial entrepreneur with 30 years of ups and downs. His current chapter is all about mentoring and helping entrepreneurs avoid needless failure. He serves as the Entrepreneur in Residence at a local university and his experiences over the years helped form the tools in this book and in the ROOT app. Colin's passion for helping entrepreneurs called him to build a business accelerator focused on the UN's Sustainable Development Goals, as well as co-found a crowd-funding platform which allows entrepreneurs in developing countries get micro-loans and helps break the poverty cycle.